D0211367

Things
I Learned
from
Knitting

...whether I wanted to or not

Stephanie Pearl-McPhee

Storey Publishing

*The mission of Storey Publishing is to serve our customers by
publishing practical information that encourages
personal independence in harmony with the environment.*

Edited by Deborah Balmuth
Art direction by Mary Winkelman Velgos
Text production by Jennifer Jepson Smith

Cover design by Mary Winkelman Velgos
Cover illustration by Dan O. Williams
Hand-lettering and interior illustrations by © Sarah Wilkins

© 2008 by Stephanie Pearl-McPhee

All rights reserved. No part of this book may be reproduced without
written permission from the publisher, except by a reviewer who may
quote brief passages or reproduce illustrations in a review with appropriate credits; nor may any part of this book be reproduced, stored in
a retrieval system, or transmitted in any form or by any means — elec-
tronic, mechanical, photocopying, recording, or other — without written
permission from the publisher. For additional information, please contact
Storey Publishing, 210 MASS MoCA Way, North Adams, MA 01247.

   Storey books are available for special premium and promotional
uses and for customized editions. For further information, please call
1-800-793-9396.

Printed in the United States by R.R. Donnelley
10 9 8 7 6 5 4 3 2 1

Library of Congress Cataloging-in-Publication Data

Pearl-McPhee, Stephanie.
   Things I learned from knitting — whether I wanted to or not /
Stephanie Pearl-McPhee.
      p. cm.
   ISBN 978-1-60342-062-4 (hardcover w/ jacket : alk. paper)
   1. Knitting. 2. Knitting — Miscellanea. 3. Knitters (Persons) —
Miscellanea. I. Title.
TT820.P3748 2008
746.43'2 — dc22

                                                    2008005462

This book is for my mum,
the clever and formidable (but non-knitting)
Bonnie McPhee.
I love her.

Introduction

Despite the way it makes non-knitters look at me like I'm a few sheep short of a flock — I have often remarked that I think knitting is an excellent metaphor for much of life. Whether we like it or not, becoming knitters changes the way we think, feel, process information, and interact with the world around us. In short, I believe knitters — by simply engaging in knitting, learning what it has to teach us, and looking at how we learn it — somehow become different from other people.

There is a school of psychology called "cognitive psychology" that concerns itself with how your brain handles mental processes like language, memory, problem solving, and reasoning. To illustrate the concept, these psychologists imagine your brain a little like it's a computer: Information goes in, is somehow stored, is accessed when you need it, and then is reused. People who research this sort of thing are interested in how you *filter* what you will focus on, the way you use *pattern recognition* and *object recognition,* and the way you experience *time sensation* — all those things that influence that computer-like processing. Now, I'm no knitting cognitive psychologist, but it struck me right away that if I did happen to be one, I would have instantly recognized these four areas as being all about the knitting.

Attention and filter theories are the ideas surrounding how you focus your mental energy. In a vivid, busy world, this is about how you will sort the hundreds of pieces of information coming at you at once and decide what you'll pay attention to, store, recall, and use. In knitting terms, you use this skill when you count out loud to drown out the kids as you're casting on, struggle with choosing one yarn that you love out of the many in the shop, or show the remarkable ability to consistently ignore the instructions for working a gauge swatch that appears at the top of every pattern. It is the skill you're using when you can peacefully set aside everything around you — the dog, the kids and the pot burning on the stove — while you knit in the living room, interpreting a chart.

Knitters use *pattern recognition* every time we knit. At a higher level, pattern recognition is what's happening every time you notice that you're decreasing along a center line and don't have to count anymore or when, after five hours of struggling with the instructions for a particular stitch, you finally experience that moment when it comes together and you understand where the whole thing is going. You're also using pattern recognition every time you make a stitch. The simple act of making one stitch after another is a pattern, and internalizing that pattern is what makes knitting easier over time and lets you know when you've arsed it up.

Object recognition sounds simple, and it is: It's the skill that your brain uses to tell a tree from a face or to recognize your car keys when you need them. You'd have a really hard time getting around without using this skill at its most basic level. In its more complex forms, you're practicing object recognition when you identify garter stitch, even though this time it's blue and on a hat instead of last time, when it was green and on a sweater. (That's way more complicated than it sounds.) It's how you can tell that your decrease is wrong and how your brain knows that your sweater isn't working out. It doesn't look like a sweater.

All of these cognitive theories are interesting, but none as interesting as *time sensation.* Even if they don't know the name for the concept, people talk about this all the time: the idea that the passage of time can feel different according to what you're doing or what you're experiencing. It's the genesis of the phrase "time flies when you're having fun" or, to put it in a knitterly context, why the plain black, garter-stitch scarf you loathe seems as if it's taking forever while the much bigger sweater made from a yarn you adore moves like lightning. Knitters play with our brains and time sensation all the time, actually using knitting to change how we feel about time's passage. I know that

I am deliberately altering my sensation of time when I'm knitting while waiting for an appointment, and I know that if you don't let me knit while I wait, that time will slow down and I'll just about go raving out of my tree.

If cognitive psychology is about all these things, and about how these things change how you store, retrieve, and use information, then surely, it must be obvious that engaging in knitting has to shape your brain and how it works. All these years I've maintained that knitters are hooked up a little bit differently than everyone else . . . and maybe I haven't been wrong or joking. Considering all this psychology stuff, it has to be true that I was right in the first place, and what we have always suspected is true: By virtue of playing around with all these brain functions on a daily basis, knitters are learning lessons and changing all the time. Knitters are actually becoming different from ordinary people.

When I add all of this up, everything I've read about the human brain and everything I know that knitting has beaten into my brain over the years, I am left thinking that there are really only two things I could do with the lessons I've learned from all this wool: I could go back to university, bust myself getting a PhD and become a really kick-ass cognitive psychologist or I could write a book about what knitting has taught me.

I went with the latter . . . and here it is.

the 1ˢᵗ thing

Beginning is easy, continuing is hard.

I THINK IT'S A FEELING every knitter knows. I am unclear why it happens, but I've seen it triggered in myself and others by exposure to new yarn or a perfect pattern or even by watching my knitting friends start something I covet. Occasionally, it happens when I'm stash storing or tidying (which we all know can trigger all sorts of maladies caused by a dreadful overdose of wool fumes).

It's startitis: the almost overwhelming urge to start a new project or ten or twenty, regardless of what's on the needles now and how much you love this current work. There's an almost itchy feeling when you get it, and a great many knitters are forever pulling themselves back from the brink of being stricken down. Startitis is often misunderstood as some sort of disapproval, a negative response to what you're currently knitting.

People think you must start turning a longing eye afield because you're bored or because your current project (or projects; a monogamous knitter is a rare thing indeed) isn't working out, or they think that you're going through a troubled patch in a project. People assume that if you're starting something new, you must be trading up due to a short attention span or a sudden urge to engage in a flighty woolen love affair.

Knitters know how it looks to others, this constant parade of new projects. We know it makes us look as though we lack loyalty, faithfulness, follow-through — or even commitment. It makes us look as though we have no sense of continuance in a relationship, and most of us even feel guilty about it. Most of us, when considering a new project, feel at least a pang of regret for work abandoned. Some of us (even though there are no knitting police and we could start twenty thousand projects a day if we wanted to) try to "do better" or work on being a monogamous, "one project at a time" knitter . . . as though there was some sort of moral victory in resisting the urge to do more of what we love.

This needs to be understood: Startitis is not a rejection of the things we are knitting now, although I do understand how a perfectly good half-finished cardigan could take it this way if you toss it in the corner like it is a dirty wash-rag just so you can start a sexy new silk pullover. Instead of a rejection, however, startitis is actually an embracing. It's all a matter of looking at the big picture.

Constantly taking up with (and rejecting) a series of projects may look as though the knitter in question is a smidge on the unfaithful side if, by a smidge, we mean that the knitter is making Don Juan look like a paragon of devotion. Yet it's not faithfulness to an individual project that should matter, but faithfulness to the art of knitting overall. By exposing ourselves to as many projects as we can, we're actually strengthening our bond with and relationship to knitting, which is, after all, all that matters.

Or at least that's what I'm telling myself. I've just started another three sweaters. 🐑

5 things
I'D RATHER DO THAN
SWATCH FOR MY NEW PROJECT*

1 Get a spinal tap.

2 Scrub the bathtub after all three of my daughters have come home from "sandbox day" at the park.

3 Babysit two-year-old triplets while simultaneously diffusing a bomb.

4 Bathe a cat.

5 KNIT MY NEW PROJECT.

* *I will swatch though, and I will even try to enjoy it, because gauge is important, darn it, and it's the right thing to do . . . even if it works only half the time because swatches can't be trusted.*

the 2nd thing

Patience is a virtue.

IT IS ABSOLUTELY TRUE that knitting involves patience. A beginner's plain garter-stitch scarf, to choose a simple example, contains in the neighborhood of twelve thousand stitches. Clearly, at some point, patience is involved. No human can repeat the same action twelve thousand times without some dose of patience, and we haven't even begun to examine what sort of fortitude it might take to pull off a sweater or an afghan. Most knitters will giggle themselves stupid, however, when a layperson unacquainted with the nature of knitting announces that he doesn't knit because he lacks the patience for it. This is what I've learned from knitting:

- You don't knit because you are patient. You are patient because you knit.
- It isn't that knitting is only possible for those who are already patient. Patience is granted

to those who knit by virtue of knitting's basic nature.

If you doubt this to be true, I suggest you try a small scientific experiment. First, take a knitter. Just about any will do (though it's probably best to get one who is relatively happy with her project right now, because messing with a knitter who's doing battle with a tricky bit is not only unfair, but can be downright dangerous). When you have one, ask her to wait for a plane. Make the wait at least an hour, and warn the knitter that there will be a period of waiting. Observe her. Left to her own devices, the knitter will pull out a project and amuse herself happily for the full hour, perhaps even expressing some regret when the period of waiting is up. She'll be the very picture of patience — and for all the world it will appear that patient people knit. After all, we can see knitting and we can see patience.

Now, take the same knitter and ask her to wait for another half hour. When she pulls out her knitting, take it from her. (Warning: Accomplishing this may require more than one scientist.) When you've removed the knitting, observe the knitter. Stripped of her coping tools, the same knitter who just displayed so much forbearance will now display not only painful knitting withdrawal symptoms, but a marked absence of patience. She may pace. She may attempt to read magazines or a book, but it won't go well. She will express restlessness and discomfort. It's even possible that a knitter who has no natural patience of her own and was relying entirely on the artificially generated patience granted by the act of knitting may attempt to drink heavily, become a nuisance to others, or even require sedation. (In the case of the truly impatient, it's best not to approach the knitter; instead, administer the sedative via blowdart from a safe distance away.)

In short, the knitter will prove my point. Knitting grants the virtue of patience . . . and without our knitting, knitters are mere impatient mortals like everyone else. 🐏

Knitting is still trying to teach me . . .

THAT MAKING BIG MISTAKES WHEN
YOU'RE LEARNING IS HOW IT GOES.
IT IS WHY KNITTING CAN UNRAVEL
(AS MANY TIMES AS YOU NEED IT TO).

the 3rd thing

Be careful what you wish for.

IN MY PRIVATE, HOPEFUL HEART of hearts
(and I know I can't be the only knitter who has
thought this) I have a secret wish: to injure a
lower limb.

Now, if this hasn't occurred to you yet, I
know it sounds crazy, but try and imagine it for
a minute. I'm not a masochist; I don't enjoy pain,
so I don't really want the injury to be something
permanent or painful, just a mild and slow-to-
heal injury to my foot or leg. Imagine going to
the doctor with a vague and minor ache in your
knee and being told that the only cure, what
you simply must do, is sit down and rest for six
weeks. Surely, as a knitter, you can see where I'm
going with this.

I want just enough of an injury that no matter
how much I want to — because heaven knows I
want to — I simply wouldn't be able to do all of

those things that, as much as I love them, eat up
knitting time. Things like washing the kitchen
floor, going grocery shopping, doing the laundry or scrubbing the toilet. (I'm sure that, like
me, you'd feel especially sad about not being able
to scrub the toilet.) Imagine six glorious, guilt-
free weeks of sitting and knitting (in my best
version of this fantasy, it's the six weeks before
Christmas), and now ask yourself if wishing for
a sprained ankle is really so wrong?

A while ago, I met a knitter who, in a terri-
bly unfortunate incident involving her husband,
poor judgment, and a car door, had found herself
in exactly this place. In early November, she got
a cast on her foot and began a knitting marathon
of epic proportions. She couldn't go to work, she
couldn't do the housework. . . . there was nothing
she could do but knit. She knit and watched old
movies. She knit and listened to the radio. She
knit with her foot up on a pillow in the sunroom
and watched birds at the feeder in the morning
sunshine. It was wonderful, because she had very
little pain, and the fantastic bonus (this really
is too much to hope for) of a husband who was

responsible for her injury and thus exceedingly guilty, attentive, and kind. He brought her tea in the morning and wine and dinner in the evening, and in between his loving ministrations, she knit.

It was, I thought, the best thing that could happen to a knitter. I was jealous — very jealous — right up until two weeks into her fortunate and fantastic knitting jag, when she was on her way to her stash for reinforcements. She tripped on her crutches, pitched forward wildly, and in a horrible, terrible moment which she regrets to this day . . . she instinctively put out her hands to break her fall and . . .

She broke her wrist.

I take it all back. I forgot the Fates have a sense of humor. Be careful what you wish for. 🐏

the 4th thing

Everything is funny as long as it is happening to someone else.

ONCE YOU'VE BEEN A KNITTER for a little while . . . like, say, ten minutes . . . the odds are very good that you will have been screwed over by knitting enough to be able to see that some of the ways it messes with you can be pretty funny. Admittedly, as Mark Twain said, "Humor is tragedy plus time," so the more time has passed since you got screwed, the more likely it is that you've been able to move through the pain and find humor in it.

Knitting teaches us quickly that our screw-ups aren't the end of the world. After all, it's only your time and sanity that are wasted when you make massive mistakes in knitting. As a matter of fact, knitting can help teach us all to manage mistakes better and learn to laugh at ourselves. For most of us, knitting will provide more than ample experience and opportunity for learning how not to take our errors too seriously (no matter how stupid they are).

The problem, though, is that time. If you have been the victim of your own temporary lack of intelligence, then the amount of time it will take to recover and laugh at your mistake is going to be directly related to the amount of personal pain you endured as a result of that error.

I once entirely botched a hat at 2 AM on Christmas Day. It was supposed to be a gift that would be unwrapped later that day, and I didn't read the decreases right and while I was trying to knit my father-in-law an elegant winter hat, I ended up with a thing that was more like a massively mutant cone-head headdress. (Hint: My father-in-law isn't a mutant cone-head.) I still can't explain how it got so far out of hand without me noticing, but I blame fatigue and eggnog. It was horrifically traumatic. Christmas Day was dawning, all the stores were closed — I couldn't buy another gift to replace it. No matter how I looked at it, or how fast I worked, there really wasn't going to be time for a re-knit. I had to go gift-less with a bad hat and an explanation, and the embarrassment of that awful day has stuck with me. I confess: I still don't think it was funny.

If, however, the bad thing that happened to you happens to someone else, even if it wasn't then (nor is it now) really, really funny that it happened to you, most knitters will be unable to control themselves. They'll have at least a wee chuckle at their fellow knitter's pain. I know several otherwise lovely knitters who still giggle when they think about that mutant hat I made. Even I think (through my pain) that watching somebody knit sleeves that don't match without noticing until she tries on the finished sweater is like watching a version of the Keystone Kops or the Three Stooges. It's knitter's slapstick, and it can be darned funny.

All we ask of each other as we knitters navigate this sometimes weary path is that if it's a really big knitting boo-boo and the pain is fresh, maybe all of you could laugh behind our backs . . . just until the pain fades a bit. 🐑

4 things
THAT ARE REALLY FUNNY WHEN THEY HAPPEN TO OTHER KNITTERS

1. A knitter comes to knit night and, for diagnostic purposes, shows her rather stunted heirloom lace shawl-in-progress, and all of you watch in horror as she comes to understand that she's missed an instruction. Although she's worked every row of the chart meticulously, she's somehow missed a line of the pattern: "Chart shows only even numbered rows. Purl all odd rows."

2. A knitter proudly displays the parts of her finished sweater, all ready to be sewn together. As she smooths her hands over her work in satisfaction, she realizes with increasing distress that she has knit the front in a size large, the back in a size small, and sleeves that are neither.

3. A knitter (who shall remain nameless, but it might have been me) pops her brand new tank top over her head and realizes that if the neckline falls so low that her breasts (both of them) are entirely visible, there may be some issues with strap length.

4. When, after six hours of cursing and attempting to sew together his new cardigan, a knitter discovers that the reason it won't go together right is not because he can't figure out where the seams go . . . but because he has knit a back, two sleeves, and two right fronts.

the 5th thing

Don't worry, be happy.

THERE ARE, I HEAR, knitters who are happy, relaxed, and accepting of all things in their knitting. When a hand-painted yarn "puddles" while she knits it so that all of the blue falls squarely upon the right breast (and only the right breast) of her sweater, she can smile and enjoy this random element of a random yarn. When a pattern with bobbles turns out to have a cluster that falls directly on her midsection, the relaxed knitter doesn't rip it back while fuming with indignation about how not a single person alive could look attractive with seven woolly belly buttons. This sort never rips back a sleeve cap nineteen thousand times because she has not yet achieved perfectly matched decreases, and she's seldom seen thumbing knitting books at 2 AM with a scotch in hand, driven to drink by her failure to generate a purl stitch that's perfect in all ways.

No, no, these knitters are easygoing. When a self-striping yarn makes a pair of socks that are fraternal rather than identical, they don't start over. If they run out of yarn at the end of a project, they might use another color and thoroughly enjoy the resulting stripe. They've never once set fire to a project as punishment for persistently possessing the wrong gauge after seven real tries. When it all goes wrong for this sort of knitter, they smile beatifically and say serenely, "It will fit someone."

Not even in a dark moment has this knitter sent a knitwear designer a victim-impact statement describing in precise detail the ramifications a small pattern error had on their lives. (They have especially never done this drunk at 3 AM.) They have never shoved a project into the back of the linen closet, needles and all, and pretended to the rest of the world that it never happened. They don't tell people that a difficult yarn was stolen out of their car, and they've never burned a baby blanket at midnight because it didn't come up to standards.

These knitters are knitting for the joy of it. They aren't driven to create perfect knits or master every technique that they hear about — or at least if they are, they aren't sobbing and destroying evidence while they do it. These knitters have a relaxing hobby, and these knitters take pleasure in all that they create.

I am not one of them, though I meet them all the time, and the funny thing is that they seem just as fulfilled by their imperfect knits as I am by my pursuit of near-perfect ones. I guess I could chalk it up to personality differences, but I think it's something else, another thing that knitting has taught me: The act of knitting is unlike almost any other human activity in that two people who are as different as camels and cantaloupes can take the same pattern and the same yarn and do their own thing with it, and both of them can walk away happy. If you are the sort who is relaxed about your accomplishments and simply enjoys the lovely act of working stitches without pressure, knitting is perfect for you. If, on the other hand, what makes you happy is rising above challenges and doing it with precision and obsessive perfectionism, then you'll love this business of sticks and string just as well.

Remarkably, knitters can shape the same hobby, the same techniques, and the same equipment to meet their personal need for perfection. There's more than one right way to knit, and you don't have to be perfect or even good at knitting to have it work out for you. That's pretty unusual, because there really aren't a whole lot of other hobbies where you can relax, be imperfect, and still have a wonderful time . . . just ask rock climbers. 🐑

5 *things*
WORRYING NON-KNITTERS
HAVE WARNED ME ABOUT

1   Knitting needles are very pointy. I could put out my eye at any moment.

2   If I were knitting while in a car and there happened to be an accident, I could be impaled or even killed by my own knitting.

3   If I am not very, very careful, I or someone else could become entangled in my yarn and be unable to elude or escape danger.

4   If I am a victim of a crime or terrorism, my knitting needles could be grabbed and turned against me as a weapon.

5   If I'm sitting and knitting in the presence of children, one of them could run into my knitting while playing and be impaled, have an eye put out, become entangled or, heaven forbid, all of the above.

    Over the past thirty-four years as a knitter, I've been warned about these possibilities many times by many different non-knitters with some degree of variation and I have to admit, it makes me a little nuts. Everything is dangerous if you

think about it (especially if you have an imagina-
tion), and most things are way more dangerous
than knitting.

In 2006, *National Geographic* published a
"Ways to Go" chart, which spelled out the odds
of someone dying as a result of various turns
of events. (Naturally, the *National Geographic*
people admitted that the chance of dying is 100
percent; it's only how you go that was examined.) According to the chart, for instance, the
chance that you'll die of cancer is 1 in 7, but being
killed in a motor vehicle accident ranks 1 in 84.
Accidental electrocution is pretty dangerous at
1 in 9,968. There's a 1 in 62,468 chance that you
will be killed by legal execution, which turns out
to be (rather unbelievably) more likely than dying
in a flood, which is 1 in 144,156. Although I've
experienced very small injuries as a knitter, and
once my husband took a needle to the foot when
I left a sock in progress on the floor, in my lifetime of knitting I've never, ever, not even once
heard of a knitter who lost an eye, was treated for
a life-threatening impaling, or was actually killed
by her knitting. I think it might be time for non-
knitters to stop worrying quite so much about the
vague and imagined dangers of the hobby and
start to be concerned about the real dangers of
knitting: moths, running out of closet space, and
addiction.

the 6th thing

Wishful thinking is only that.

I AM OFTEN RUNNING A LITTLE LATE, and this morning was no exception. I was scrambling around the house to grab my wallet and knitting bag before my buddy Rachel showed up to get me. We were headed for the Knitters Fair (if you don't live near one, you're not living), which meant about three hours of driving there and back. We were going in Rachel's car, which thrilled me to no end, since it meant she would likely drive both ways while I scored some primo knitting time. I was rushing to organize two unwound skeins of sock yarn before she came. I rammed the first skein onto my swift, found the end, attached it to the ball winder, and started turning the handle as quickly as I could. Whipping along, I cursed, an eye to the clock. Here I was again.

I often have trouble prioritizing when it comes to leaving the house. Though I had my wallet, my knitting notebook, my knitting bag and I was taking care of winding my yarn for the trip . . . I was not yet wearing pants, which, in my experience, is a pretty important part of leaving the house. Knowing that Rachel likes it when I wear pants when we go out together, I wound only one of the skeins and then dashed upstairs, claimed a pair of pants, yanked them on, whipped downstairs, heard Rachel pull into the lane, grabbed my stuff, headed for the door and . . . stopped.

Should I wind the other skein of yarn? What if, with all this car-knitting time, I finish the first sock and then I'm in the car with nothing to knit? I headed back for the ball winder and the other skein. Rachel honked. I turned back toward the door, reasoning with myself. It takes me seven to ten hours to knit a dress sock, depending on the size and complexity, NOT one and a half hours, not even three hours. Never. I don't knit that fast, never have, never will, never could. There was absolutely zero chance that I would run out of yarn on the way there or on the way back. I turned toward the door again. Rachel was still honking, and you do not want to come between that lady and the Knitter's Fair.

Yet my inner knitter stopped me dead again: What if you knit faster than usual? What if you stop for lunch and knit in the restaurant? What if the car breaks down and you have hours and hours to knit and no more yarn than that one skein? "What if," my knitterly psyche screamed. . . . What if?

There is no "what if," I told it, I have ten hours of knitting with me, and I am going to a Knitter's Fair, where, if I've changed my mind an hour and a half from now, I will be able to buy more yarn — lots more. There is no reason to make Rachel wait while I wind yarn I don't need and can't possibly knit up in the span of today. I do not knit that quickly. I do not need the other skein. Firmly, then, with emphasis and real confidence, I opened the door, stepped through . . . and shouted, "Hey Rachel, gimmee a minute!" and returned to the ball winder.

There's no point in arguing with my inner knitter. Besides, it's sort of flattering how fast she thinks I knit. ꒰ᵕ̈꒱

the 7ᵗʰ thing

Winners never quit
(or why I should win all fights with my knitting).

- Knitting has only two stitches: knit and purl.
  All knitting is completed using these two
  lowly stitches and some instructions. I know
  both of those stitches, so there is simply no
  reason why I shouldn't be able to take whatever challenges knitting can dish out.

- I am a grown-up. Knitting is not the boss of me.

- My knitting patterns are in English. I read
  English. Despite their more than occasionally cryptic nature, the instructions for this
  project are actually written in a language I
  allegedly speak fluently. It just can't be that
  hard, especially since my pattern book is
  called *Easy Knitting Patterns in English That
  Anyone Can Do.*

- I have an army of knitting friends who have
  battled their own knitting demons and who
  will be more than willing to help me in a bit-

ter duel with any given project. They have fought and been burned by knitting in the past and they have endured staggering knitting frustration and failure. Far from beaten, they have prevailed against the minions of knit that strive to have us all insane and sweaterless. Knowing my pain, they will be on my side. Whatever their struggles, they have conquered knitting (some days) . . . and one of them has just got to know how to do a damned buttonhole.

- Knitting is a time-honored and mystical pursuit. Turning string into wearable, three-dimensional objects is something that's been done by millions — no, hundreds of millions or even billions of human beings who have knit before me. Shepherds in the sixteenth century knit while they tended flocks. The samurai soldiers of Japan knit their own socks and gloves. Seventeenth-century nuns, Victorian ladies, soldiers recovering from injury in both world wars, even little children in sweatshops: All of these knitters came before me, and they knit with less instruction, fewer references, very little in the way of yarn shops, and absolutely no high-speed Internet access. They did it because they had to, because there was no other way to stay warm or get the things they needed — and darn it all, none of them quit. Quitting your knitting just wasn't an option unless you had another plan for fending off frostbite and darn it all. . . . If they could do it, I can too.

the 8th thing

You can't make a silk purse out of a sow's ear.

A LONG TIME AGO, when I was a very young mother, someone gave me a gourmet cookbook that contained a recipe I'd enjoyed at a dinner at her house. The recipe was for a fantastic mushroom stroganoff that I thought was one of the yummiest things I'd ever eaten. I hurried to the grocery store to buy all the ingredients, but there was one problem: I couldn't afford them. I decided to make do. I bought substitutes that wouldn't blow my whole week's grocery budget on a single meal. It called for cream; I used milk. It called for portabella and shiitake mushrooms; I used regular button mushrooms. It called for butter; I used margarine. The wine? I substituted water. I painstakingly put together my version of the stroganoff, and was absolutely devastated when it was a pale (and sort of gross) imitation of the glorious dinner I had eaten at my friend's.

I explained the outcome to my mum, telling her that I must not have the skill at cooking that my friend had. I proposed that I just needed practice making the dish. My mother looked at me, poked dully at the puddle of milk and margarine on her plate, and proclaimed, "Darling, practice all you want, but you can't make a silk purse out of a sow's ear."

What she meant — and she was right — is that your end product can be only as good as the materials you start with. Despite learning this when it comes to cooking, I've had the hardest time learning it with knitting. I'm forever admiring a beautiful sweater in a magazine, gasping at the price of the suggested yarn, and then being absolutely flabbergasted when, after I substitute a less beautiful yarn to save money, I get a sweater that's less beautiful too. ("Less beautiful" is actually too kind. Some experiments have been downright unwearable.)

Not to be taken for a yarn snob, I know that there are exceptions. Certainly, all of us have seen a knitting project that was deadly good despite being knit with dollar-store acrylic (some of us are even fortunate enough to be the knitters who pulled it off). I myself made a jacket for my mum out of dishcloth cotton that has turned out to be her very favorite of all time. Being a knitter who knit through her student years (and her one-income, three-baby years), I also have a pretty good grasp of the concept that all of us are going to have times when we really can't afford something better and have to knit the crap because it's a lot better than not knitting at all. Desperate times call for desperate measures and all that. I don't have a problem with cheap yarn, and as a matter of fact, I'm glad it's there so that I'm not reduced to knitting my own old pantyhose cut into strips or making the most of an old roll of kitchen string I found in the back of a drawer — though in the right hands (just not mine) I bet those have potential too.

I am just glad to have finally learned that I didn't get the sweater or the stroganoff I expected not because I am an incompetent and everyone else is more skilled than I am, but because sometimes, if you start with crap, that is what you will end up with. 🐏

the 9th thing

You gotta roll with the punches.

I FLY A LOT. I KNIT A LOT. As you can imagine, because flying is a sitting-down, boring sort of activity, I try to combine flying and knitting as much as possible. For the most part, I knit happily on flights from here to there, but I'm always aware that I am not the one in charge, that if someone in a uniform tells me that I can't knit (even if I checked the airline's guidelines not less than three hours earlier and printed out the rules to show the staff, rather desperately, the part that says that knitting needles are absolutely fine) — that if they aren't comfortable — I will have to give up, and worse . . . I'll have to give up without a fight. The airlines make the rules, and there is nothing we can do about it. If we want to use the service they provide, we're going to have to do it their way and learn to roll with the punches a little bit.

Once you do get your needles on board, you may face other challenges. I've had flight attendants ask me to put away my needles for fear I'll impale someone in the event of turbulence. (I've given this a lot of thought, by the way, and I think that if there was enough turbulence that people were at risk from my knitting needles, the flight would have much bigger worries than little old me and my sock-in-progress.) I've had flight attendants worry that there may be a bump and I'll put my own eye out. I've had other passengers tell me they're uncomfortable with anything pointy on a flight. I've even had one or two ask me if security let me on board with my needles. (I have always been unclear as to how they think I would have managed to avoid security.) I even had one flight attendant tell me she worried that there would be some rough air, that this rough air would surprise me . . . and that during this moment of extreme surprise, I would let go of my knitting needles, which would then fly knifelike through the air and impale one of my fellow passengers in a tremendous and gory episode which I would certainly regret.

At this, I thought hard. My needles were bamboo circulars and very light and fragile. I thought about what sort of "surprise" would be required for me to hurl them with that sort of force, and I thought about explaining all of this to the attendant.

Then I remembered that on her airplane, she makes the rules, and I have to attempt to roll with the punches. I put away the knitting, but I couldn't help but notice that the guy next to me had a very pointy metal pen that he was using to fill in the Sudoku game in the in-flight magazine, and I considered that if he were "surprised," that pen could have gone flying too — and being about 100 percent heavier and sharper than my needles, it was a far more dangerous thing. If my small pointy sticks had to go, then I wanted the other small pointy sticks tucked away too.

I didn't say this though. I didn't say a thing. I rolled with the punches. I got some airline wine from the cart, and I thought of a solution: I hope I get that flight attendant again, because I'll be the lady knitting with pens, and there'll be nothing she can say about it.

5 things

THEY DON'T TAKE AWAY FROM YOU IN AIRPORT SECURITY THAT CAN REPLACE KNITTING NEEDLES IN AN EMERGENCY

1 Chopsticks

2 Coffee stir sticks

3 Pencils (pens too, but they are less good)

4 Toothpicks (but you can only make very small things)

5 The handles of wooden spoons (but you can only make big things)

10 things
A KNITTER CAN DO ON AN AIRPLANE INSTEAD OF KNITTING

1 Drink or eat (a lot)

2 Read about knitting

3 Write about knitting in a knitting journal

4 Look at yarn catalogs and plan knitting

5 Talk to the people around you about knitting

6 Ask to be sedated until you arrive at your destination and can be reunited with your knitting

7 Crochet (sometimes the airlines are less threatened by hooks than needles; while I understand that crochet is not knitting, it at least has the yarn element, which can reduce withdrawal symptoms)

8 Take a portable DVD player with you and watch instructional knitting DVDs

9 Read a regular book (I think this would work; I see other people do it all the time)

10 Try to knit anyway, seeing what sort of progress you can make with pencils and the cords from twenty-three airline headsets

the 10th thing

Babies grow.

I FEEL TERRIBLE POINTING OUT this simple truth that knitting has taught me, but I've seen so many knitters burned by it that I can hardly not. I thought it was obvious, but when I see knitters (myself included), acting like they have no idea of the cruel realities of baby expansion, I feel I would be remiss if I did not write it here. The considerable charm and diminutive size of babies makes them frequent targets for our knitted love — but babies don't just grow, they grow fast. To add insult to knitterly injury, the smaller they are, the faster they grow. Therefore, please consider these significant points before casting on a wee layette to bestow on the next eight-pound human who crosses your path.

- A human baby generally doubles its birth weight by six months and triples it by a year. This means that any sweater knit for a new baby has a brief lifespan of usefulness. Babies grow fastest in their early months so the smaller the object, the less time it will be used. This may be discouraging to some knitters. Conduct your knitting accordingly.

- Many babies, being non-knitters, feel strongly that hats, booties, and tiny mittens are a vile encumbrance. A baby seldom enjoys these garments as much as the adult who provides them. If you are the sort of knitter who really needs to see the recipient of your work enjoying your creations, you may be knitting up the wrong tree with babies. Most of them are willing to strangle themselves to remove an adorable bonnet or are willing to make a life goal of whipping booties off their feet and onto the floor.

- Babies are, to put it as delicately as possible, leaky . . . If you're going to be offended if someone leaks something smelly and staining onto your work, you may want to wait a little while before presenting your knitting to parents. The incidence of leaks in human young diminishes after a few years.

- Even with the best warning available to humanity and all its experience and science, you will have no more than nine months notice to knit your gift. If you're a slow knitter, you may want to knit something in a bigger size. Despite all attempts by billions of pregnant women, due dates remain nonnegotiable.

If none of this bothers you, then you are one of us: the brave, the true, the knitters who in the face of all adversity, know their hard-won knits will be outgrown, flung, dirtied, and possibly underappreciated, but still look fondly upon these tiny people and think only that one item, so carefully handmade, deserves another . . . even if the recipient is going to puke on it. 🐑

Knitting is still trying to teach me . . .

THAT THE KNITTING MUSES
HAVE AN EXCELLENT, IF CRUEL,
SENSE OF HUMOR.

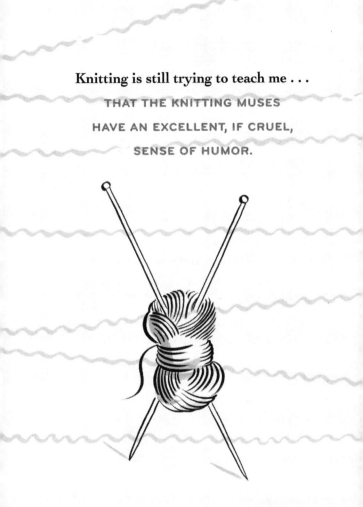

the 11th thing

Good things come in ~~small~~ packages.

LIKE MOST ARTISTS, I support my work with an extensive and varied collection of the materials I use to create. Picasso had paint; Michelangelo had marble; Mozart had piano, pen, and paper. As a knitter, I have yarn.

Now, I'm way past feeling bad about how much yarn I have. I used to think I had "too much." For a while, I even tried going on a yarn diet to try to lose a few pounds of fiber, but the truth is that my heart was never truly in it. Really, I was just saying all the things I think non-knitters want to hear. We've all been there. They want us to acknowledge that we have too much yarn, to admit that we're out of control and that we should have less. They talk to us about *obsession* and *hoarding.* They fail to see the big picture.

The way I see it, the big picture is that painters have paint and canvas, gardeners have plants and acreage, carpenters have wood and tools — and even if you want to think of knitting as a hobby rather than an art form, golfers have clubs, golf balls, carts, green fees, memberships, and entire golf weekends for their hobby.

Once I put my collection of yarn into perspective, I realized I didn't care what people thought. I really didn't. I cared whether or not I had room for yarn (spiritually and literally), I cared about whether or not I could afford it, and when I ordered that big box of fancy wool from Germany, I even went so far as to consider my daughter's possible feelings about my intention to store it in her closet. (I admit I would have considered it for a longer time or more in her favor if she'd ever cleaned a closet, but I digress.) I took a good look at the stash, and I realized that I wasn't hurting anyone, that I wasn't spending money I didn't have, and that I certainly wasn't spending more on yarn than the golfer down the street was spending on his golf trips, and I stopped feeling bad about it. Not only did I stop feeling bad, I started buying yarn whenever I took a fancy to.

I must admit that removing the element of guilt about having so much of the thing I love has increased the influx of it somewhat, but I don't mind. This is the stuff my art, my hobby, and my life is made of, and I'm just not going to support the idea that having a lot of wool is a crushing, world-important issue worth discussing with non-knitters. This is the yarn I'll have for the rest of my life. It turns out that knitting has taught me that good things come in all sizes, and the size doesn't matter, as long as you're happy with what you've got.

Now, where I'm going to put it all — that's certainly open for debate. 🐑

the 12th thing

Three men can keep a secret if two of them are dead.

IT IS A WELL-KNOWN FACT that there are some secrets that are just too juicy for anybody to keep. For example, there's no chance that your neighbor and her husband can take up nude bathing in their backyard pool and reasonably expect that the neighbors with a clear view are going to be able to keep it to themselves at the next community barbecue. It's just too good not to tell. Similarly, you simply never can tell two knitting friends about a huge yarn sale and expect they won't pass along the good news to two more (or twelve) of their favorite knitters. It's not reasonable. Go to the sale and get what you want before you spill the beans.

Secrecy is a delicate thing, and while friendships are a sacred trust . . . half price merino is going to be a deal breaker. 🐑

the 13th thing

Practice makes perfect.

UPSTAIRS IN MY HOUSE, in the very back of
the linen closet, behind the sheets and towels, are
several pieces of my old knitting. They are in the
back, packed up tight where people (including
me) are unlikely to see them. They are terrible
— absolutely, viciously, breathtakingly terrible.
Truly, they're embarrassingly bad. In fact, they're
so bad in so many ways that it is impossible to
narrow down exactly which offenses of knitting
make them so bad.

It could be that I chose the very worst of all
possible materials, selecting for only economy
rather than quality, since I was young and poor
and I didn't understand that unless you're a mira-
cle worker, if you start with crap you end up with
crap, no matter how expertly you knit the crap.
Speaking of things that are expertly knit, these
are definitely not. They have bizarre and random

increases mid-row that somehow involve an extra stitch (or ten) and rows in which I decreased away those extra stitches, thinking that this was a brilliant way to deal with them and restore order. (It isn't.) One of the sweaters is so poorly knit that it has a neckline I executed with all the skill of a clutch of drunken emus. Worst of all, every single one of these errors is compounded brilliantly by the fact that when I knit these monstrosities, I seem to have had all the color sense and good taste of a blind showgirl on an acid trip.

Now, time has passed and I have become a good knitter, having learned a great deal since I knit those early abominations. I've gained skill and understanding, I've learned that gauge matters and that there are some colors that don't look good on me (or any human, really), and I know enough now to correct my mistakes as I go along instead of knitting them into permanent infamy. I am so much better at knitting now, that sometimes, when I'm putting away towels and I catch sight of those early knits lurking in the back of the closet, I think about getting rid of them — throwing them away or donating them to charity.

(Actually, nix that. Some of the people who get their clothes from charity have enough problems. Getting my mutant knitwear could only make things worse.) I'm rather proud of the knitting I do now, and I shudder to think of someone finding this stuff after I pass away. When I'm feeling prideful, I don't want these to be the artifacts I leave behind. I think a person should be remembered for her best accomplishments, not her lapses of knitterly judgment — or sanity.

These moments though, are misplaced conceit. I don't seriously want to throw away my old stuff. When I really think about it, these horrible knits are exactly how I want to be remembered: as a person who got better with practice. When I think about all that I felt skill-less at — parenting (the first time I picked up a baby that was mine, I couldn't believe they'd given an incompetent like me this responsibility) and writing and marriage — I look at those incredibly crappy knits and I think about how awful I was and how much I've learned. Even though I screw up all the time and make horrible mistakes and feel as though everyone in the world is better at everything than I am, I can look at those horrendously bad pieces of knitting, then look at my knitting now, and remember. Everybody gets better with practice. Knitting has taught me that, and knitting is the proof. I can be taught. I'm a good learner, and I'm keeping those knits for the next time I have trouble remembering that.

Thinking about it now, though, maybe I'll put a little note on them. If I drop dead I don't want people to think I knit that way on purpose. 🐑

the 14ᵗʰ thing

You can fix almost anything.

I AM THE WIFE OF AN INTELLIGENT and engaging man, as well as the mother of three bright, creative girls with high self-esteem. These fine qualities make the man exasperating and the children difficult, but assuming I survive them, they are a lovely family with high entertainment value.

My husband wants me to run rapids in canoes (I can't tell you how many times in my life this will likely get me wet and bruised), and I've had to talk him out of rewiring the whole house for high-speed Internet access with nothing more than his instincts, a library book, and big plans to knock out a couple of walls. I can't count the number of things he's "improved" until they don't work. After many years together, I've only just now managed to convince him to at least glance at a clock a few times a day.

The children, taking after the man mentioned above, have wanted to move to Belize when they were fifteen, climbed bookcases as babies, organized uprisings at school, and repainted their bedrooms in garish colors while I was at the grocery store. (My children are both sneaky, and fast.) They have tried to start small businesses which involved selling my belongings, experimented vividly with dye, and once, in an incredible and sparkling test of my motherly affection for them, had a water balloon fight . . . in the living room.

Now fortunately, I'm a bright and engaging woman with a fair bit of get-up-and-go, and most days I can take on this bunch of maniacs pretty well. I've grounded my kids for trying to get passports, I've installed fire extinguishers throughout the house, I've established that under no circumstances is it okay to rappel off a staircase (even with a safety harness tied to the bathroom door), that blowtorches are only for people old enough to vote, and that no home renovations are to be undertaken — even if all four of them agree that they should add a fourth floor

— without my express permission, even if it is true that it would be a grand surprise for me.

I tell you all of this by way of explaining that in dealing with these people around me, as a person of passion myself, I am liable to make the occasional error. When there is a lot of passion for life involved, as well as a lot of passion for remaining among the living, things can get a little heated. As the person charged with keeping this whole bunch alive and out of jail, I acknowledge that I may sometimes approach the upper limits of acceptable volume while firmly explaining the way things are going to be. Like all parents, it's inevitable that I'll screw up sometimes, and when I do, I can end up feeling as if I tanked the whole wife or mother thing.

Luckily, I am a knitter, and from knitting I have learned how to handle my mistakes. I can go to the person I screwed up with, sit quietly on the edge of their bed, and say, "I'm really sorry. I'd like to rip back the last ten minutes and have a big do-over."

Mostly, starting over works just as well with people as it does with knitting. 🐑

Knitting is still trying to teach me . . .

THAT KNITTING A REALLY BIG THING IS
LIKE BEING MARRIED FOR A LONG TIME:
YOU HAVE TO FIND A WAY TO DO THE
SAME THING OVER AND OVER AGAIN
WITHOUT WANTING TO TRASH IT FOR
SOMETHING NEW, EXCITING,
AND BETTER-LOOKING.

the 15th thing

It takes a great deal of pressure to make a diamond.

AT SOME POINT, EVERY KNITTER will be presented with opportunities for skill growth. These opportunities will often be disguised as "knitting deadlines." Even knitters who don't enjoy deadline knitting and find it so stressful that it takes all the fun out of the thing can occasionally have one come up by accident, even with the best planning.

Sometimes gift-giving occasions like Christmas or your mum's birthday sort of sneak up on you (despite the predictability of these events arriving on the same day every year). Or maybe your best friend's due date arrives in what seems like a whole lot less than nine months and leaves you with twenty-three days of baby-blanket knitting to accomplish in mere hours. Often, the culprit is a case of knitter's high self-esteem; we grossly underestimate how long it will take us to knit something. We all make timing errors with our knitting, and the consequences, though occasionally ugly, emotional, and damp with tears, reveal that knitting challenges, like other life challenges, often teach us that we are capable of much more than we had ever expected.

A few years back, in a misplaced gesture of fondness for my sister, I decided to knit a pair of kilt hose for her rather unworthy, bagpiping boyfriend. Kilt hose are an undertaking: They are traditionally knit at a pretty fine gauge, go up to the knee of the kilt wearer and then have a fold-over cuff, just to increase the amount of knitting required. Fortunately for bagpipers, but unfortunately for the knitter, most bagpipers have two feet, so a knitter must complete this feat of derring-do twice in order to get a pair. At the time I was not much of a sock knitter, but I had knit a pair or two and I figured these couldn't be that much harder. I was wrong. Those kilt hose took forever — or what seemed like forever — and because I approached them with a lot more confidence than turned out to be appropriate, I ended up with a crushing knitting deadline. It all came down to me and the kilt hose at midnight for many nights in a row. Had they been for someone I liked, I would now regret the curses and ill will that came to be knit into them during those trying midnights. As it was, my sister dumped the lout, and now I sort of like the fact that he's wearing all that bad karma.

In retrospect, as mind and finger numbing as the experience was, I now have to admit that it completely changed an aspect or two of my knitting. For starters, I now think of regular socks as short, and having knit what seemed like acres of fine-gauge work, I'm now far more likely to take on any project at that gauge. I walked away from those hose thinking "Good riddance to bad rubbish," but there is no denying that I'm a better knitter for it, and I advanced my skills, whether I liked it or not.

There are knitters and some ordinary people (like the ones who say that I take on crazy projects to create stress because I enjoy it, which has never sat right with me) who will claim that pressure isn't good for people, that pressure amounts to stress and discomfort and that because knitting is supposed to be relaxing I shouldn't let it get crazy. To them I point out that pressure and knitterly heat can transform a knitter, much like exerting pressure and heat on carbon creates diamonds. Knitters, like regular people, can discover new and wonderful qualities in themselves as they rise above during times of duress. There is seldom greatness without great effort.

It is probably not a good idea to remind anyone looking difficulty in the eye that it takes 1,500 degrees Fahrenheit, pressure of more than 850,000 pounds per square inch, and a very, very long time to turn carbon into diamonds. The wisdom is probably going to be lost on them while they are sleep-deprived in the middle of an endless pair of kilt hose for a bagpiper they don't even like, but surely you can see what I mean. 🐑

the 16th thing

You can't win them all.

I WAS STARTING A NEW SWEATER, or trying to. Straight out of the gate though, I misread the pattern and cast on the wrong number of stitches. That didn't bother me; it happens all the time. I chalked it up to user error and cast on the right number of stitches, but after a few rows I discovered my gauge was too loose. I unraveled my work, switched to smaller needles, and immediately cast on the wrong number of stitches again.

A sweater can hardly be blamed for my stupidity, so I took some cleansing breaths and cast on the right number of stitches only to discover that my gauge was now too tight. I ripped back, found my needles in the middle size, calmly retrieved the other needles from where they'd landed when I hurled them across the room, and tried again. Now I was getting the right stitch gauge, but discovered that I wasn't even close on row gauge. I decided I didn't care. I would compensate later. (I wasn't sure quite how, but I didn't let that stop me.) I knit the ribbing for the sweater bottom and switched to larger needles, just like the pattern told me to . . . except that I must have taken leave of my senses for a second or two because I only swapped out one of them and then proceeded to knit about four inches of the sweater with two markedly different needles.

When I noted my error, I decided for some insane reason that a glass of wine might take the edge off. This might have been true, but because I next placed the waist shaping at the front and back of the sweater instead of at the sides, it's possible that the decision to have a second glass may have affected my accuracy. The third glass made it so that I didn't care.

The next morning I fixed the shaping and proceeded to knit to the armhole. I followed the instructions carefully. Only when I'd finished the armhole opening did I remember that way back at the beginning I'd decided to reject all concern for row gauge. Now though, I had neglected to compensate for that shortfall. In following the instructions, I had created an armhole opening so tight that I was going to have to rip it back again or accept that this sweater would make my fingers all go numb and a little blue when I wore it.

I ripped it back again (after perhaps stomping on it once with a few choice and unladylike words, for which I can hardly be blamed) and took the sweater to the backyard to knit under the trees and regain peacefulness. Events went much better out there. This almost made up for the fact that I left my knitting on the garden table overnight — where it was not only rained on, but was also unceremoniously crapped on by a bird.

As I stood there, looking at the decoration on this sweater that was . . . let's be frank, not working out at all, I wondered if I would be able to forgive the sweater all of this. The mistakes, the ripping, the gauge, the rain, the missing rows, the errors in the pattern (that was later): Perhaps it was too much pain to pass between a knitter and her sweater. I wondered if I would be able to let go enough to love the sweater, or maybe if I would love it more because I'd surmounted all of the troubles and risen above the challenges. I wondered if my feelings for the sweater would be like my feelings for my children, where surviving the difficult times had only endeared them to me more.

Though knitting has taught me, generally, that all is well that ends well and that rising above adversity (mostly) strengthens the sense of accomplishment, this time it taught me something entirely unexpected. The acids in bird crap will totally destroy wool.

the 17th thing

Size doesn't matter.

IT IS A SAD TRUTH that most knitters have a very poor body image. (This is likely because most human beings have a very poor body image, and most knitters are human beings, but I'm just guessing.)

Non-knitters struggle with body image, believing themselves to be what they're not — fatter than they are, thinner than they are, taller than they are, or far more beautiful than they imagine. All of us have ended up standing stunned in a clothing store trying to understand how we could have been so wrong about the relationship between our arses and our pants. But because knitters make some of their own clothes and because how they make their clothes is so unpredictable, knitters have special issues with body image. A huge number of knitters are out there wearing knitted stuff that doesn't come anywhere close to fitting them properly.

It should be easy. Knitters should buy or design a pattern, measure themselves, select the right size from among the choices, knit that size and there you go, it's off to the races. Right? Wrong. Enter a litany of knit-based influences that results in most of us knitters at least occasionally looking like we've never seen ourselves in a mirror.

Gauge. Every knitter knows that while gauge can certainly be predictive and that theoretically, if we select the 38-inch-chest pattern and knit a gauge swatch and get the correct number of stitches to the inch, darn it all, the sweater should be 38 inches around. Every knitter also knows that there's a 50/50 chance that something will happen to gauge along the way and that our sweater could, for no reason other than the fact that it's a Tuesday, turn out much larger or smaller than predicted. Now, a knitter can wear a sweater that is too big, even if it isn't attractive, but because a sweater that is too small is utterly hopeless and unwearable, a knitter will often opt for a larger size "just to be sure." The result can be a knitter proudly wearing a sweater that swells upon her body like the mainsail of a grand schooner billowed out in a full and hearty wind.

Patience. While knitters really want items that fit, they're also only human, and when making a thing drags on for a while, there is a natural human tendency to shorten the effort and move on to the next temptation. This results in a knitterly knack for occasionally overestimating how much of a sleeve has been knit. (Admit it: How many times have you tugged just a little bit while measuring?) Knitters also convince themselves that a sweater will lengthen in the wearing or otherwise contrive a way to believe that whatever they're knitting, they have knit it long enough. Though they are loathe to admit it, this explains the preponderance of ¾-length sleeves, cropped sweaters, and skimpy scarves. Flattering? Maybe not . . . but the project got done, darn it, and at the time, done was all that mattered.

Pride. After hours and hours of knitting, it would be a rare knitter indeed who couldn't reach deep into his psyche in order to put on (or insist that another human put on) his magnificent creation. I don't know about you, but more than once my pride in my well-executed cables have been enough to get me to put on and go out in a sweater that was otherwise horrendous.

In case you haven't been adding all of this up, the sum total of all these knitterly quirks means that the next time you see a knitter wearing an odd garment that doesn't fit (remember, that may be you in the mirror) just add it up. The sweater is too big around because you can put on a too-big sweater, but not a too-small one. It is too short because his next sweater beckoned; and no matter how it looks, that knitter is wearing it anyway, darn it, because his pride in his accomplishment and the fifty hours of invested knitting effort are simply not going to be overlooked . . . Fashion be damned. Knitters hold clothes to a different standard. To knitters, clothing is also art . . . and besides, size doesn't really matter. Right? 🐑

Knitting is still trying to teach me . . .

TO COUNT. I THOUGHT I HAD
MASTERED IT IN THE FIRST GRADE,
BUT SINCE I HAVE JUST PLACED
THE NECK OPENING FOR A SWEATER
DIRECTLY OVER MY RIGHT SHOULDER
BLADE, I APPARENTLY NEED TO
WORK ON IT.

the 18th thing

Nothing is perfect.

I AM A PERSON WHO LOVES PERFECTION and control, although I suspect I would have a really hard time convincing anyone who has ever seen my housekeeping, wardrobe, or hair of that. It seems to me that most of the time, the search for perfection is at best exhausting and at worst, hopeless. Trying to gain control is even more hopeless, because it turns out that almost everyone on the planet is not under my direct influence, no matter how much easier it would be for me if they were.

Despite my abject failure to perfect and control humanity, I've discovered one aspect of my life in which it's possible to perfect and control everything: my knitting. Knitting is a relief to type-A people — those of us who like to demand certain standards in things — because it is entirely inert. Knitting has no feelings that can be hurt if you curse it for failing you. Knitting won't cry at its desk if you tell it that it isn't performing up to your standards. You can be as absolutely picky as you want with your knitting, and no one will suffer. Yarn is almost infinitely reuseable. You can rip back and reknit something as many times as you want to, tinkering with stitches and edges, obsessively choosing decreases that match each other perfectly. Whatever need for perfection and control any of us may have can truly be met by knitting, without doing any damage to anyone's self-esteem. And that, my friends, can't be said of anything else in my life.

If I had things my way — which, we have already established, I do not — the whole world would work the way knitting does. I would be in charge, I would say what happens and when, and I would be able to quit anything that wasn't working out or had stopped being fun — without having to live with the consequences. Knitting is perfect for those of us who have these urges to control everything but have learned that spouses, coworkers, children, and friends cannot be managed in this way if we still want them to be our spouses, coworkers, children, and friends. It would seem prudent that people with control issues learn three lessons: to let go, to lighten up, and to find an acceptable outlet for the times when those first two simply aren't possible.

I humbly suggest knitting to moderate the desire to run the world, and run it right. The satisfaction that perfect garter stitch can give you or the solid feeling of well-being that comes from being able to make all the decisions (if only on a small scale) can be a very good outlet for the intense and engaged knitter's heart.

Knitting is also a whole lot easier than divorce, finding a new job, going to family therapy, or suffering eventual loneliness, which is where I would be headed without it. Knitting's moderating effect on my personality also explains why, occasionally, when I'm a little wound up . . . people sometimes suggest I go knit for a while. 🐑

the 19th thing

Two heads are better than one.

I STARED AT THE TV. I WAS STUNNED. There's this rancher in Cuba, Raul Hernandez, who's worked his arse off inbreeding cows until he has finally arrived at what he wants. After carefully selecting cows that have the qualities he desires, then breeding them and selecting the most promising of their offspring, and then breeding the offspring, he's finally managed to produce — get this — *vacas de patio*. Translated from the Spanish, that's "patio cows."

These cows are being bred for their teeniness, and now this rancher has cows that stand only a miniscule 23 to 28 inches tall. These dog-sized cows eat grass and weeds, and theoretically, you could keep one on your patio or in your back-yard and it will produce about 4 quarts of milk a day, depending on the patio cow in question. That's a lovely supply of milk for a family. Raul was talking about how they could supply fresh, organic dairy to families who don't have access to a store and don't necessarily have the resources or the desire to manage cattle.

My mind reeled. Patio cows? This was brilliant. I turned to my husband and said so. He smiled at me and asked me if I wanted to go to Cuba and get myself a little wee cow. I stared at him. There are moments in this marriage when I would have to say that he doesn't know me at all. I've got no use for a patio cow. I can get milk at the corner store, for crying out loud. I'm thinking outside of the box. I'm taking the fine work of Raul Hernandez to its next logical step. The man is a genius at the beginning of a beautiful arc of an idea.

I wonder if I could call him. I don't know about this little cow idea, but just imagine . . . patio sheep — not those miniature sheep that are bred without knitters in mind, but real fleece sheep, like, say, patio Shetlands or patio merinos. Wait . . . patio llamas! Patio alpacas! Patio cashmere goats!

This is brilliant. I've got to call Raul Hernandez, because together (since I don't know anything about sheep breeding, and I'm not sure I want to learn) we are going to make a million dollars.

Raul and I are going to be a great team. *Oveja* is Spanish for sheep, right? Somebody look up "llama." This is going to be fantastic. 🐑

the 20th thing

Honesty is the best policy.

Famous lies:

- The check is in the mail.
- I didn't inhale.
- It's not you, it's me.

Famous knitting lies:

- That sweater pattern is "one size fits all."
- You will absolutely have enough yarn to finish.
- That yarn is machine-washable.
- The technique is obvious. You'll have no trouble.
- It took two hours to knit.
- I did swatch and I did get gauge. 🐑

the 21ˢᵗ thing

Pain for beauty.

MY MOTHER AND I DISAGREE ABOUT SHOES.
We agree about a very great many other things,
such as politics, that raising teenagers is a challenge equal to climbing Mt. Everest (though at
least an Everest ascent doesn't take as long), and
that dusting is a despicable chore and a waste of
a fine woman's time. But despite being of a common mind about nearly everything else, I cannot
see her point about shoes.

My mother owns a lot of shoes. She likes
them. She shops for them, spends money on
them, knows the difference between a sling-back
and an espadrille, and has an opinion on what
to wear with any pair. She can fiercely debate
toe shape (open, snipped, square, or pointy) and
thinks that heel height and type (stiletto, wedge,
shaped, or common) is an important decision that
a person should make daily. My mum has shoes

that go with only one outfit and says things like, "Look at those strappy sandals! They're divine." She can no sooner walk by a shoe store without going in than I can pass a yarn shop.

Much to my mother's shame, I own only four pairs of footwear: sandals for summer, short boots for spring and fall, snow boots for the dead of winter, and a pair of neutral-colored dress shoes for weddings or funerals that demand them. I don't care for shoes. In fact, if it was possible to live in a big city barefoot, I would. While my mother's priority is fashion, mine is comfort, and shoes, no matter how strappy or elegant or wedge-heeled, simply aren't comfortable to me.

"You should accept that there may be pain for beauty," my mother tells me, but I just can't go there. I simply can't agree that we should be more uncomfortable to be more beautiful. I'm willing to be a little less beautiful to be a lot more comfortable . . . and me and my clunky sandals tramp through life holding this to be true. I maintain that I will not suffer for vanity and that I'm not like my mother in this respect . . . or at least I thought I wasn't, right up until last Wednesday night, when I was leaving to meet some knitting friends at our weekly knit night.

It was a hot August evening, the sort we get here in Toronto that practically steam, yet as I headed out the door, I stopped to pick up and put on my heavy wool cardigan. I had just finished it, and heat be damned, I was going to show it off . . . . It's a beautiful piece of knitting, let me tell you. "Wool?" my mother quipped, a smirk on her lips. "It's a thousand degrees out, silly girl. You'll have heatstroke before you get to the corner. What happened to your position on vanity?"

I thought about it. I was sweating, over-dressed, uncomfortable, and . . . still reluctant to take the thing off. It turns out that I might now understand "pain for beauty" a little bit, but only when it comes to hand-knit sweaters. I still don't get the shoes. 🐏

the 23rd thing

If you are patient in one moment of anger, you will escape a hundred days of sorrow.

— Chinese saying

I AM PRETTY SURE that lace knitting is the best value in the knitting world. If we think of knitting and the money we pay for it as part of our entertainment budget, then lace really is the best bang for your buck. In general (though there are some exceptions that can burn a hole in your wallet faster than a night at a casino with free drinks), yarn is sold by weight. This means that 100 grams of worsted weight wool is going to be somewhere in the neighborhood of 220 yards. Because it's so much thinner, 100 grams wool laceweight is probably going to run about 1,000 yards or more, while not being much more expensive. Add to your figuring the fact that because of the patterns and general fiddling it requires, lace takes longer to knit and it won't take a rocket scientist to figure out that what you're spending per hour of knitting entertainment is going to be a lot lower for lace. Toss into the mix the fact that you'll be creating an heirloom that will knock your own socks off, and suddenly, you can understand what so many knitters see in lace.

Now that I've offered this compelling evidence, I feel that in the interest of knitterly honor, I must warn you that there's a downside: While this is one of the best knitter's tricks around, lace knitting has a much higher chance of costing you your sanity and leaving you feeling as though you're a few jalapeños short of a zippy salsa . . . if you catch my meaning.

Those of us who've fought and won have learned what's important to know about lace knitting. First, because lace is all about not just your stitches, but the way you make them, anything related to your technique that you have always done in your own quirky way is now going to matter a lot. For instance, if you've never been really hung up on whether your decreases lean left or right and you start knitting lace with that attitude, you might be headed for a world of disappointment.

Second, because lace has a pattern that usually "stacks" on top of previous rows, you can't fudge anything. If, like me, you usually just knit two together if you find you have an extra stitch at the end of a row, your lace is going to be out of alignment pretty quickly, and that's going to make you crazier than a bag of wet cats. Lace is a precision game.

Finally, everything I've written about lace up until now — the fineness, the pattern, the precision — ends up meaning that unless you're a lace-knitting machine with no human failings at all, you're going to end up tinking from time to time. This is perhaps the greatest challenge of lace. Those of us who just yank out the needles and rip back until the world makes sense again — that's not always a good option with lace. It's delicate, it's precise, it's an exercise in patience.

Knit lace. Knit lots of lace, but breath deeply, accept the joy of precision and the rewards of forbearance and restraint, and, above all, remember to read the quote at the beginning of this advice. You'll likely need patience in more than one moment of anger. 🐑

the 23rd thing

There's no accounting for taste.

I WAS HANGING OUT IN A YARN SHOP, a rather common place to find me, and had set myself up with a cup of coffee and my current project, a particularly beautiful aran sweater with intricate cables. Two ladies came in and started surveying the shop, taking particular note of my knitting. They proceeded to have a conversation about it which I could plainly hear. (We can discuss at another time why on earth two people would have this conversation with me right there, but I suppose they thought I was deaf.) The first knitter looked at my work from across the room and said, "Man, look at that sweater. Cables are so ugly."

Now, I try to be understanding. Really, I do. To each their own, beauty is in the eye of the beholder and all that . . . but to say cables are ugly? I inhaled slowly, then released my breath evenly. I tried to absorb what I'd heard. Cables are ugly? All cables? Rope cables on ganseys? Tiny cables up the sides of socks? How about the staggering variety of fisherman's sweaters or winter toques with warm and lovely knots knit all around? She didn't like all cables? Every cable ever knit? I was so stunned that I was shaking inside. Hundreds of years of inspiration, cleverness, and thoughtfulness . . . and she stands there, declaring a whole genre of knitting "ugly"? How could she possibly tar all cables with that one brush? There was a whole world of possibility out there, and while you can say, "I don't like most cables" or "I don't like to knit cables" or "I think cables on most sweaters are a mistake," how could you think every single one is ugly? Sure, there are cables that are heavy-looking, and in chunky yarn they can be a lot of texture to absorb, but to dislike all cables in every incarnation ever knit? How closed-minded and narrow a knitter was she?

I ranted on like this for a while in my head, imagining a litany of things I'd say to her if only I dared open my mouth. If I was braver, I'd show her the socks I was wearing, with a clever and delicate cable rib at the cuff. I'd whip a particularly lovely pattern book off the shelf and force her to look at all of the cables within until she admitted that she'd been hasty. I'd tell her that until she had looked at every cable ever devised, she could not, in all fairness, make the sweeping generalization that "cables are ugly."

It turns out (lucky for her) that I am not that brave. So my ugly cabled aran and I sat in stony silence, trying to telegraph my opinion of such a biased and insulting knitter through the air. After a while, she sat down and took out her knitting, a sweater with great masses of bobbles down the front, and I suddenly caught myself thinking it.

Bobbles? Bobbles are ugly. I hate bobbles. If you knit bobbles on the front of a sweater, they look like nipples. Furthermore, multiple bobbles down the front of sweater make it look as though you're equipped to nurse a litter. No wonder she doesn't care for cables. She's a bobble knitter!

Seconds later, my brain caught up with me, and I was properly ashamed. Pardon me. I don't know where that came from. Bobble on, dear knitters — and to each their own. 🐑

the 24th thing

The truth will out.

I ONCE MET A KNITTER WHO, when she ran out of yarn money, made a bold choice: Flat out of yarn, she had taken her birth-control money for that month and bought the yarn she needed instead.

I was stunned. Being a woman (and a mother) of some experience, I pointed out to her that this choice seemed . . . risky. As a general rule, the consequences of skimping on birth control are cute but expensive. I've got three teenagers who have ended up being pretty hard on the yarn budget.

She laughed then, and stated the simple truth. She and her husband weren't going to need birth control that month. She had looked through her life for what she could do without for thirty days . . . and it wasn't yarn. 🐑

the 25th thing

If at first you don't succeed, try, try again.

MAYBE IT'S BECAUSE KNITTING has such a rich and varied history. Maybe it's because so many knitters have finished projects that prove they're successful (this point can be demoralizing if you're not currently enjoying knitting success). Or maybe it's because knitting was considered child labor until the turn of the century (and remains so in some parts of the world). Most knitters will eventually come to believe that there is very little they can't accomplish in knitting. They might not be able to do it now, they might not be able to do it for some time, but generally speaking, if a human possesses the intelligence and hand-eye coordination to read and write at a minimum level, then he is capable of being a darned solid knitter.

Knitters are of two minds when it comes to telling people the truth about how easy knitting is. On the one hand, it's great to hear all of those people say, "I'm not smart enough to knit" or "I could never do something that hard." It's empowering that they all think so highly of us. If they believe that it takes a special gift to knit, then it follows that they think knitters are smarter than they are in some ways. Frankly, with all of the disrespect knitters get dealt sometimes, I have to admit that I quite like that they think knitting is too difficult or would outwit them. It's like my own personal revenge for all the times that people have giggled at me for my plans to spend a wasteful afternoon knitting while they were on their way to a golf course.

On the other hand, I think highly enough of knitting that I can be a bit of a missionary about it. I'm never going to stand in an airport wearing a hand-knit sweater and handing out balls of yarn, but I do enjoy spreading the word of knit far and wide and often feel compelled to urge others to try it if they show even the slightest bit of interest. In this process, I often tell them the truth: If they dressed themselves today, they're smart enough to knit, and if their clothes match, they're smart enough to knit well. I toss in that I have faith in their ability to learn, because if my six-year-old can make a potholder, then a grown-up who regularly fires up a computer or operates a car can totally pull off a garter-stitch scarf. Heck, I bet she can even make a hat to go with it. I remind them that everybody feels dumb and awkward about new things in the beginning, and that they can learn to knit as they learned everything else. I show them what I used to make and what I make now. I tell them that it turns out that there's not much difference between a scarf and a lace shawl, once you get going. I'm reassuring, I urge them to try, and I offer to show them.

Then I remember that if I am successful in convincing them that it's not hard and they do become knitters . . . they are going to be competing for some of the world's yarn supply. In my next life, I'm going to try to be a better person, the sort of person who doesn't shut up about the wonders of knitting when she thinks about creating competition. 🐑

the 26th thing

There's more where that came from.

I SUPPOSE IT IS WISHFUL THINKING, justification for all the time that I spend knitting, but I am sure that knitting is teaching me life lessons all the time. I believe that humans learn best in small ways and that if they need to grasp a larger concept, it helps to have it illustrated first on a small scale. Knitting is downright excellent for this. Need to learn that work pays off? Knitting's a grand illustrator. Trying to grasp the concept to be prepared at all times? Buy more yarn. Internalizing "appearance isn't everything"? We knitters learned that lesson when we loved a hideous scarf we made ourselves just because we made it ourselves. Knitting is a fountain of teachable moments.

I don't know why, then, but the one thing I can't seem to learn from knitting, despite ample opportunity, is the idea that "there's always more where that came from." Anyone would think that after decades of dedicated yarn buying, watching yarns come and go over the years, I would learn that just because a yarn is discontinued or scarce or special to me doesn't mean that I need to buy it up and hoard it like a squirrel with obsessive-compulsive issues, trying to shield myself against the day I can't get more. If I see that a yarn is discontinued and on a sale table, just the idea that it's going away forever makes me want it.

I worry. I worry that I will miss it. I worry nobody will ever make another yarn I like as well. I worry that the person dying the yarn so beautifully will herself die. I worry I will run out of money and won't be able to buy yarn in the sad and distant future. I worry about global warming affecting sheep so that they don't grow as much fleece. I worry that this will make yarn too expensive and then I won't be able to afford it. I worry that this yarn I love will be the only yarn I ever love and that for the rest of my days I will regret not having it. I worry about this despite always finding a new yarn that I love just as well as the one that I swore my undying allegiance to mere moments before.

The truth, is that yarn is sort of like a high school boyfriend. While you're with him, he seems to you to be the most beautiful and wonderful man, and you know you'll never find anyone else like him nor survive in a life that doesn't contain him. Then, after the breakup and a tub or two of ice cream, you find out that there's another one you like just as well . . . or even better.

I know this, I really do, but when I see that yarn I love, lying there on the sale table for the last time ever, half-price and lonely? I just can't shake the feeling that there really might not be more where that came from.

Knitting is still trying to teach me . . .

PATIENCE. ENOUGH SAID.

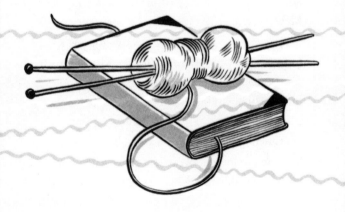

the 27th thing

Speak softly and carry a big stick.

THERE ARE UPSIDES AND DOWNSIDES to having a finely honed stash. All knitters experience times of retarded cash flow. Having a good stash around the house is sort of like having a highly personalized yarn store where you can shop for free. Stashes are a creative source, a fountain of inspiration and the genesis of many a fine project. But if you let a stash get the upper hand, that advantage can become a massive complication.

Owning a spectacular yarn collection can become a source of pressure. Many a fine knitter has crumbled under the psychic weight of the stash and ended up its servant, casting on and off as the stash dictates, starting project after project after falling victim to the multitude of offerings her stash can make. For a knitter with low stash resistance, a big cache of yarn can feel almost like a burden — the weight of innumerable unknit skeins pressing down on the knitter while screaming "Pick me! Pick me!"

Some knitters handle this pressure by deciding not to have much of a stash at all. They buy as they go and keep little in reserve. These knitters are likely to have one of those handy "jobs" or "careers" that provide them with a stable yarn budget. Then there are those knitters who, like me, require a stash to support them through the lean times and feel that, for the most part, stash ownership is inspiring. These knitters need to manage the pressures of the stash through self-discipline and by keeping the stash at bay.

It has taken me years to learn that I am the boss of my stash. My stash is there for me to pick and choose from, to be inspired by, and for me to use as I see fit. Of course, there are still times when I go into the stash to get one ball of sock yarn and emerge with plans for two sweaters, a hat, and a set of mittens, as well as a slightly dirty feeling, but with practice, I now rule the stash.

Mostly. 🐑

To: *The Stash*
From: *Stephanie*
Re: *Your behavior of late*

I know that you and I have an important, loving, fluid relationship, and mostly I treasure you and the way you respond to new yarns and changes in how often I visit. (I really appreciate how you dealt with that mohair thing. I'm so sorry about what happened.) That's why, after all this time together, I dislike having to lay down the law like this, but you leave me with no choice.

You seem to be under the impression that we are in a marriage of equals — that I will love, honor, and cherish you and that you will take part in our relationship as a teammate and partner who makes suggestions and decisions about the life we lead together and what gets knit around here. That, my wooly friend, would be wrong.

You are actually more like my high-priced concubine. I love and cherish you, feed, house, and spend money on you, and in exchange, you're to give me what I pay for: entertainment, pleasure and silent, nodding assent. I'm the one with plans, and you exist only to please me. I demand that you cease and desist with the following unacceptable stash behaviors.

- Stop throwing sock yarn at me just because I've finished something. This behavior will not be tolerated. You can also quit wagging your fancypants yarns at me and tossing skeins off the shelf, for I will not be tempted. I am going to finish the socks I have in progress before I want to see even one more label about "hand-painted" anything.

- Please leave the door to the stash closet closed the way I left it. I know you force it open sixteen times a day to give me a tempting peek inside because you resent my decision to finish my current sweater before I knit anything else. Having made that decision, I am reminding you that I am simply not the sort of knitter who would open the closet to look at the gray merino sixteen times a day (actually, I was just looking for the tea towels), so back off. I know it's you who opens the door to make me look weak, because frankly, I'm better than that.

- Immediately stop with the whispering about other projects that would be more fun than everything I have on the go right now. I bought you, I own you, and I will make the decisions here. (You, there — the mouthy laceweight in the back — shut it.)

I want you to know, my darling stash, that I believe in your basic goodness and that I think you are a reliable and decent collection of yarn. I would never have brought you that nice silk for your back corner if this wasn't true. I hope this review of appropriate stash conduct helps us continue our long and fruitful relationship. You are a mighty stash, and I admire the way you stick to what you want, but no matter what, you still need to learn . . . no means no. 🐑

the 28th thing

Make hay while the sun shines.

I SAVED UP AND BOUGHT A KIT for a sweater I
very much wanted. It was knit from two strands
of yarn which you alternated back and forth
throughout the whole thing. Strand A is a mohair
bouclé. That means it's loopy and bumpy and
hairy, which, because you can hardly tell where
your stitches are with this stuff, should make it
a Class 1 knitting mistake hazard. Strand B is a
super-fuzzy brushed mohair, which means that
it's effectively a yarn adhesive. The combination
of a Class 1 knitting hazard and a yarn adhesive
means the potential for looming disaster with this
sweater is painfully obvious.

Having suffered terrible indignities at the
hands of projects like this before, I looked at
those two yarns and understood instantly what
was at stake. There was going to be no going
back. Loopy bouclé yarns don't rip back well;

fuzzy, hairy yarns really don't rip back well; and loopy bouclé yarns worked together with fuzzy, hairy yarns effectively weld together in the knitting as if they are the yarn equivalent of Super Glue. The stitches stick to each other like Velcro, and the bouclé defeats all attempts to pull it back, forming nasty knots as you go. I knew that once I cast on, I'd better make sure that I was right; there would be no going back and little chance that I could rescue the yarn if it turned out that I had made a mistake. On a good day I make a knitting mistake every ten minutes, so I was a little threatened.

Sure, you can knit a swatch to help remove some of the risk, you can pay extra attention to the pattern and try to engage in safer knitting, but as you're gingerly moving forward with expensive yarn that has only one real try in it, the process can become the adrenaline-pumping equivalent of tiptoeing through a minefield (okay — a minefield that blows up yarn instead of people, but it's still intense). Swatches lie. Patterns have errors. Even if I was exacting, nothing is sure in the land of the bouclé-mohair sweater.

You must move forward with thoughtful, careful maneuvers, knowing every step of the way. If you're wrong about the dimensions of this sweater, if you go just one inch too far in the knitting, there will be no recovery.

You move forward slowly with this sweater, knowing full well that despite all the money, all the time, all the caution and the avoidance of haste . . . that if you screw up and make the arms too long, you'll have made a sweater you entirely adore . . . for your really tall aunt Carol.

When confronted with this sort of challenge, I've learned that I need to concentrate. I need to seize quiet, peaceful times when I can focus and I need to make the most of opportunities when I won't be interrupted. In short, I need to make hay while the sun shines . . . I need to wait until my husband is out. 🐏

the 29th thing

Look before you leap.

ONE OF THE CONCEPTS KNITTING TEACHES
you (eventually) is the idea of looking far ahead.
You have to acknowledge that the failure to look
ahead with gauge means you might not get something that fits. Failing to look ahead with timing
means you might not finish your mum's sweater
by Christmas. Not reading the pattern all the
way through before you start can have tragic
consequences. Even buying yarn demonstrates
that knitters are looking forward in time: If you
looked ahead at what you think you'll accomplish
in a lifetime of knitting, you'd stop buying the
stuff right now. This foresight is good thing in
humans, and I humbly propose that we take this
concept a little further: that we start doing a little
knitting math in this forward-thinking vein.

I examined the number of stitches in a sock
and I did a little calculating: Let's say there are

16 inches of knitting to accomplish for a sock, and that it takes about 10 rounds to add up to an inch, and that there are 68 stitches in a round. If my math is correct (and it should be; I had a thirteen-year-old check it), this means there are about 10,880 stitches in a sock. Multiplied by 2 (because, hopefully, you knit socks in a pair), this results in 21,760 stitches to knit before you will have wearable items.

(By the way, it's normal to need a minute to lie down now, having realized how many stitches you may have knit in your life so far or how many more you have planned in order to use up your stash.)

Now what if you look before you leap? What if you take advantage of that human ability to look ahead and change one or two tiny variables? What if you cast on 64 stitches instead of 68? Bingo! This results in a slightly snugger sock, but now you're only knitting 20,480 stitches to the pair. What if you make the leg or foot a little shorter? If you cut off 2 inches, you're down to a mere 17,920 !

If you're thinking that isn't a big deal, you just aren't thinking. That's 3,840 stitches less. If you still can't see the logic, go time how many stitches per minute you knit as you work one round of a sock and then look at that number again.

Looking before we leap has got to mean that suddenly, I am not the only one who's doing a bit of math and then rapidly coming to the conclusion that if it's going to save me thousands and thousands of stitches, maybe I should be checking the foot size of people before I begin to love them, and that in the meantime (since I'm already stuck with some big-footed people) my family can live with slightly snugger, shorter socks. 🐑

Knitting is still trying to teach me . . .

THAT THINGS GET KNIT FASTER
WHEN YOU ACTUALLY WORK ON
THEM. THAT'S WHY THE SCARF I'VE
ALLEGEDLY BEEN KNITTING FOR
TWO YEARS JUST ISN'T GETTING ANY
BIGGER, NO MATTER HOW LONG
I LEAVE IT IN THE BASKET.

the 30th thing

It's funny because it's true.

IT MAKES ME LAUGH WHEN PEOPLE TELL ME, as they so often do, that knitting is a silly way to get a sweater or a pair of socks. These garments are simply clothes to non-knitters. They look at the time and expense involved and shake their heads sadly at knitters' collective lack of intelligence. Even knitters can't argue that if what you're after is just some new clothes, knitting might be a pretty dumb way to get them.

After all, knitting a sweater takes time — way more time than just going to the store and grabbing one off the rack. Anybody who's recently bought yarn, especially good yarn, can attest that knitting your clothes from scratch certainly isn't any cheaper than going to the store. In fact, once you factor in what your time is worth, most of us are knitting fantastically exorbitant sweaters and ridiculously priced socks. Even if I bought sock yarn on sale and merely "paid" myself minimum wage, a pair of hand-knit socks amounts to a good deal more than the one dollar per pair I'd spend if I bought socks bulk at a discount shop.

Add to this what non-knitters don't even know (but knitters do): After you buy the yarn and the pattern and spend hours and hours knitting up a sweater (and ripping it back and knitting it up again), due to operator error, there is still a chance that the sweater won't fit or frankly, even be wearable. Knitters entirely understand the non-knitter's confusion about why on earth, if you need a sweater so badly, you don't just walk into the store, pull one in your size off the rack, and be bloody done with it.

Knitters know this. We get the point. We see what's happening. It's not as though we're uninvolved here. We know knitting is slow; we are the ones doing the knitting. We know it can be expensive; we're the ones wiping out a yarn budget. We know that if a person had a whole family to clothe and keep safe from frostbite, and if that person had serious limits on their time and budget, and if that same person lived three minutes from a discount store with socks on sale for a dollar, that knitting would be a incredibly silly way to get clothes for that family. We know.

That said, we know something non-knitters don't. We're not just making clothes. There is a reason the hobby is called "knitting" and not "sweater making." If it was just about getting a sweater, we would totally do it the way everybody else does. Who on earth would spend $20 on hand-painted sock yarn and then invest at least twenty hours of time churning out the things if there was nothing in it but a pair of socks?

What we know and try to explain is that when you knit a pair of socks, you don't just get clothes. You get satisfaction. You get art. You get a boost to your self-esteem that only comes from making things cleverly. You get hours of cheap entertainment and endless interest. Best of all, you get to have something to do while all those non-knitters stand around in their standard-issue store sweaters and talk about how silly knitting is.

And that's funny, because it's true.

Knitting is still trying to teach me . . .

THAT THERE'S NO SUCH THING AS TOO MUCH INFORMATION.

After a new knitter finished her first project, I gave her a gift: a beautiful skein of yarn. She came to knit night the next week with her first sock cast on and a huge grievance about the wool. "I don't want to seem ungrateful," she complained, "and this yarn is very pretty, but I'm finding it impossible to work with." With that, she pulled from her purse the biggest mess of fiber I have ever seen. It was about 380 yards of sock yarn, all tied somehow into one massive, near-hopeless knot. Several knitters nearby actually gasped and recoiled in horror.

I flinched with guilt. It was my fault. I had assumed this knitter knew. I had known something for so long that I had forgotten that there was a time I hadn't known, and I had skipped telling her something because it seemed like almost insulting information. In my zeal to share my knitting joy, I had just handed her this yarn, and when I did? I had neglected to tell this innocent, fledgling knitter that you have to wind a skein into a ball before you knit it.

the 31ˢᵗ thing

He who laughs last laughs longest.

KNITTERS ARE QUITE USED TO the gentle ribbing (pun intended) that we sometimes take from ordinary people. We smile and endure the persistent belief that we're engaged in some silly little pastime that is no equal to the non-knitter's clever and majestic hobbies such as fishing, bird watching, or collecting comic books. We knit while non-knitters chastise us for engaging in a grandmotherly or feminine activity. We knit while they point out that our hobby is largely unproductive (unlike collecting comic books) because they think anyone can buy the stuff we're making at any of a thousand stores. We knit with our mouths shut while they say they "wish they had that sort of free time," and we (mostly) say nothing while watching non-knitters settle into an evening of idle TV-watching. Knitters are, by and large, peaceful creatures, we simply knit and let others hold their opinions. We've given up on correcting them. (In my experience, most knitters have figured out that at least when it comes to knitting, revolt is at best time-consuming and useless, and at worst can tangle your yarn.)

There is a lot to be said for knowing in your heart that people are wrong. When it comes to being teased for knitting, it turns out that we shall likely have our revenge. Several studies in the last few years have indicated that there are certain things you can do for yourself to help prevent or at least stave off Alzheimer's disease and dementia as you age. Researchers point to activities that require sorting out clues or codes, use both hands, require some degree of memory work, involve hand-eye coordination, and generally demand mental energy. These kinds of activities will either keep the connections in the brain bright and active or help in the formation of extra connections so that if you do suffer from a neurodegenerative disease as you age, you might have some brain to spare.

Knitting is a perfect example of this kind of activity. It definitely requires both hands, it absolutely requires hand-eye coordination, it even uses both hemispheres of the brain at once. As you knit there is obviously an element of memorization as you work through stitch patterns. I can tell you that a knitting chart is definitely a code you have to decipher in order to achieve any degree of success. In fact, knitting is one of thirteen activities that a study in the journal *Neurology* suggests reduce the risk of Alzheimer's. French researchers have found that knitting, gardening, working crossword puzzles, and traveling all help to reduce the incidence of dementia and keep your mental acuity as sharp as your needles.

What all of this means is that though knitting is certainly no magic bullet for wellness in the aging brain and there's no substitute for exercise and an all-around healthy lifestyle, it's definitely beneficial and can increase your odds of keeping the brain healthy — and that means that though non-knitters may laugh at us for our silly hobby, we may very well be laughing last . . . and longest. 🐑

5 ways
TO GAIN HEALTH BENEFITS
FROM KNITTING

1   Knitting has been shown to help form new pathways and connections in the brain and it may help prevent Alzheimer's and dementia as you age.

2   Assuming you've rather got the hang of it, knitting can lower blood pressure and promote relaxation. (Every knitter knows that obviously, not all projects go down that way.)

3   Knitting results in tangible progress. All those who do it see the immediate effect of their actions and can experience measurable success, some degree of focus, and a sense of accomplishment and progress, however small. This can be helpful for those who struggle with depression.

4   Joints require motion to stay healthy. For those knitters with arthritis, "use it or lose it" remains an important notion in treatment. Knitting can help arthritic hands remain flexible and promotes a reduction in pain. (Naturally, this assumes that you are able to limit knitting and not slide all the way from "use it or lose it" to the rather uncomfortable "abuse it.")

5   Knitting can promote fitness. Who among us has not raced to the yarn store, run for a wool sale, walked a mile to find the merino we're looking for, or wrestled another knitter to the ground for that last skein of tweed that we need to finish a sweater? (Maybe that last one is just me. It was a very nice tweed.)

the 32nd thing

Idle hands are the devil's workshop.

A WHILE AGO, I MADE A TIMING ERROR related to a knitting deadline that ended up being pretty catastrophic. For reasons I won't go into here (but mostly having to do with me being an idiot) I found myself having to knit eight socks in eight days — that's eight adult-sized, sock-weight socks. Naively, I felt this was going to be difficult, but possible (a frequent knitterly delusion), and I started knitting. Being a mostly ordinary person, and because I wouldn't want to land in prison for neglecting my children, I couldn't just quit all my regular stuff and knit. I had to approach my life as usual: cooking, writing, cleaning, taking care of the kids . . . except for one critical difference. Without exception and whenever possible, if my hands were free for even a moment, I knit socks. I multitasked. In fact, I was the supreme multitasker. If I was walking, I was knitting. If I was on the phone, I was knitting. If I was thinking at the computer, I picked up the sock I was working on, even if it meant I just did three stitches. I took advantage of every little possibility.

My friends thought I was out of my mind. I think they may even have considered an intervention of some kind. They regarded me with a critical eye and assessed my sanity. Even my knitter friends thought I might have gone a little off the deep end, and more than one ordinary person called me "knit obsessed." I defended myself with historical evidence. Bishop Richard Rutt wrote, in *A History of Hand Knitting*, ". . . it is a mistake to think that the early knitting-frame quickly speeded up the bulk production of stockings. A framework knitter working hard might produce ten pairs a week, while a good hand knitter could make six."

Six pairs of stockings in a week? Twelve stockings? Admittedly, Bishop Rutt is speaking of professional knitters who worked at it for a living, but even so, if I lifted all burdens from you for eight hours a day and let you work at knitting stockings for a living, would you be producing six pairs a week? (I thought maybe I could do it for one week. Then I would die.)

He also quotes Richard Valpy (1754–1836) speaking about the stocking knitters of Jersey: "This is the chief employment of the women. The dexterity and expedition with which they dispatch a pair of stockings are almost incredible. . . . A woman seen walking without a stocking in her hand is stigmatized with idleness."

It's incredible to think of the specifics. Children as young as four were being taught to knit at this time in England, and certainly by the time they were seven or eight, they were expected to be making stockings in a way that could contribute to the family's income. Women, men, children: all knitting away at stockings, producing certainly as much, if not more than my measly sock a day, all while chopping wood for the fire, baking bread, sewing and mending clothes, knitting all the other items that the family needed to keep warm, caring for children, and in general leading an extraordinarily difficult life with far less leisure time and no DVDs.

If you contrast this productivity with my trifling idea to knit a mere sock a day, I don't think you'll see me as a knit-obsessed maniac on her way to a mental breakdown or think of me as headed for some sort of vague incident involving men with huggy coats and a sedative blow dart. All this, and sock a day starts to sound reasonable. . .

As a matter of fact, historically speaking? I might be a slacker. 🐑

5 ways

THAT KNITTING IS BETTER THAN VIDEO GAMES

1 I never, ever have to take turns with my sister.

2 I decide how many points I get and for what.

3 I can do it even if the power goes out.

4 I never lose because I forget to hit "save" before I go do something else.

5 If my mother was to come unhinged and scream, "I cannot stand the infernal sound of your knitting for one more second," I could pack it up and take it to my room.

the 33rd thing

Haste makes waste.

I'M SORT OF A FAST-MOVING PERSON. Like a lot of people who enjoy getting things done, I have high enthusiasm, bore easily and have an attention span like a hamster with ADD. As a result of these personality traits, I've really had to work at trying to learn that haste makes waste. I tried to learn this when I displayed my propensity for attempting to get where I'm going way too fast and got lost or knocked over stuff on my way. I attempted to learn this when I tried to speed up the cooking time of rice by turning up the heat and thereby immolated an entire pot-full. (This didn't stop me from trying the same technique with oatmeal. I can be a bit of a slow learner.) My whole life, everybody has been trying to teach me to slow down long enough to get a grip on something before I launch into it. My whole life, I've been screwing stuff up because I'm still trying to learn to take the time to do things right.

Knitting, which is an excellent teacher of many things, has also tried to teach me that haste makes waste. It hasn't lectured me, it hasn't told me to slow down, it hasn't put me in detention, and it hasn't grounded me. Instead, every time I've neglected to take the time to knit and wash a swatch in order to check my gauge, it's simply given me a sweater the size of a luxury ocean liner or a hat that entirely covers a human head, right down to the neck. Knitting doesn't play at subtlety.

Despite this discovery, that knitting has no problem with punishing you for rushing, and despite the fact that every knitting pattern ever written has a warning at the top to remind you of the consequences the knitting Fates may exact should your excitement for a new project cause you to forget yourself ("To save time, take time to check gauge"), I and just about every other knitter I know still ignore this warning in moments of extreme knitterly enthusiasm. We simply launch without looking, making haste with no regard for wasted time or knitting energy. We end up with yet another garment that bears no relationship to the intended object.

I've wondered why we do this. Clearly, knitting has tried to teach me this concept over and over and has done so far more effectively than my stubbing my toe as I rush though the living room, so there has to be a reason why knitters continue to ignore the warning. Having to re-knit something is a big deal: It takes a lot of time, and that should be an effective deterrent.

My guess is that because the consequences of failing to knit a swatch are only that you have to rip back your work and knit it again, there's no real incentive to learn to swatch. After all, we like knitting. Having to do more of it just isn't a severe enough punishment. 🐑

the 34th thing

Denial: it ain't just a river in Egypt.

AH, DENIAL. All of us learn the value of taking a dip in the river of self-delusion from time to time. Denial is an important bargaining tool in the arsenal of every person's relationship with reality. In the land of denial we can convince ourselves that almost anything is possible. I don't know a single human who doesn't need to deny the spiritual truth about their lives occasionally, if only so that they don't have to think about running off to Aruba when they face up to the laundry pile.

Knitters particularly need denial when:

- You're trying to finish a pair of socks for your mother's birthday the next day, and halfway through the cuff of the first one, you've managed to convince yourself that you're "almost done" and will absolutely finish in time.

- Even though you've used nine balls of yarn to complete the back and sleeves of a sweater, you tell yourself that the remaining ball "might" be enough to knit the front.

* You tell yourself that the "mis-crossed" cable right over the left breast of your sweater isn't obvious and you definitely don't need to fix it. (You do, though; we both know you will never wear it if you don't.)

* You manage to convince yourself that even though your sister's bust is 44 inches and the sweater you're knitting her is coming out a rather smaller 36 inches, that you'll really be able to "block it out bigger."

* You successfully tell yourself that sock yarn doesn't count as stash and isn't included in your yarn diet. (Hint: If it takes up space or costs money, it counts.)

* You've knit seventeen warm wool hats with earflaps because you love the pattern, and despite the fact that you live in the hottest part of Libya, which has not seen a chill since the Ice Age, and violently resist any insinuation that these hats may not come in handy. 🐑

the 35ᵗʰ thing

Everything is relative.

IMAGINE THAT A BUDDY OF YOURS tells you he's going to do something completely insane, something absolutely, preposterously stupid and dangerous, such as going skydiving for the very first time while he's drunk as a woodlouse in a rum barrel.

As a good friend, you'd be forced to say something like, "Please get in my car. I'll drive you to the hospital where you can be treated for your illness." Jumping drunk and unprepared out of a plane is right batty, no question. Now imagine that your friend reflects on your offer of hospitalization and says, "Okay, I'll take some skydiving classes before I jump, and I'll go sober." Doesn't that sound more reasonable? Of course it does. It almost sounds like a good plan. Your friend has just demonstrated relative risk. Jumping out of a plane is always risky, but jumping out of a plane with no training while hugely impaired is so risky that, by comparison, this new plan of pitching himself out of a plane 3,000 feet above the ground with his wits about him suddenly seems sort of okay. If you compare the relative risks, jumping out of a plane in this condition is much better than Plan A, which was absolutely a piece of crazy pie.

Teenagers use the concept that everything's relative to great effect. For instance, they might propose that their very solid 11 PM curfew be moved to 3 AM. Once you recover from the shock, you find yourself agreeing to midnight, because relative to 3 AM, midnight suddenly seems like a winner.

Knitters also can use this idea of relativity to their advantage. Knitting has taught me that if you're having a big knitting problem, you just have to assess it in relative terms. Imagine that you're knitting a sweater for yourself and you have a 38-inch chest. Think your sweater requires lots of work? Get a spouse with a 50-inch chest and start trying to knock off knitwear for him. All of a sudden, that first sweater doesn't seem so unreasonable, does it? Has it occurred to you that ordinary socks take too long? If you knit some knee-highs, your return to regular socks will be painless and euphoric. Are you finding a baby blanket to be a broad expanse of boring knitting? If you cast on an afghan on small needles, you'll beg for the baby blanket. Have you thought that the lace scarf you're making is fiddly and tedious? I have an heirloom lace shawl pattern you can borrow that will knock the sense right back into you. For every knitting challenge, there's a relative project that will send you rushing gleefully back into the arms of the project that was breaking your will to live before you considered the alternatives. It works every time. Shift the gauge, shift the size, shift the complexity . . . suddenly, you shift your perspective.

Are you under the impression that you'll be knitting that baby sweater for the rest of your life? Yeah. Try making a baby. It's all relative. 🐑

the 36th thing

Knitting is like marriage.

- You don't throw in the towel just because it isn't working right now.
- There is always something happening that you really weren't expecting.
- The odds are extremely good that what you end up with won't be anything like what you were trying to achieve.
- The longer you work at it, the better you get at it.
- Both marriage and knitting, as Samuel Johnson said (though he wasn't speaking of knitting), are "the triumph of hope over experience." 🐑

the 37ᵗʰ thing

Knitting teaches generosity.

I CAN UNDERSTAND THAT we knitters can look a little greedy, what with our stashes overflowing and that way we behave at yarn sales, and I know that *generosity* is not the word that springs to mind when we observe the look on a knitter's face when she's asked to part with the last of her cashmere, but I have proof.

Wait for winter, then look around. See all those people wearing knitted things? Hand-knits everywhere: little children with mittens, babies with sweaters and blankets, scores of people wearing hand-knit socks, men with hats, mothers with shawls, teenagers loafing on the couch under enormous afghans. There are a lot of knitters in the world, but there's just no way that all of those people made their own stuff. (Especially not the babies. Humans who can't feed themselves lack the hand-eye coordination to be good knitters). All those non-knitters got their garments somewhere, and because the number of people wearing hand-knits is far greater than the number of knitters, it only stands to reason that these knitters must be a very generous species.

There are many theories about what might make knitters so generous that one knitter can cover her entire immediate circle with toasty warm evidence within a season or two. One suggestion is that you don't have to knit very long to understand the special warmth and loveliness of a knitted thing, and that knitters want to share this fantastic feeling with others. Another idea has to do with knitting being a gift of time and love rather than wool, and that giving someone a hat is an expression of the time and warmth a knitter wants to share with another person. Some people think that knitting simply attracts those who are already generous and sweet, rather than converting them. (Having witnessed the dog-eat-dog mentality at a 50-percent-off yarn sale, I'm not sure I can get behind that one.)

I humbly propose another theory. Your average knitter, obsessed as we are with the art form, is quickly going to begin producing far more in the way of warm things than are needed by even an arctic-bound knitter. Knitting breeds generosity, true . . . but perhaps only because knitters better get generous in a hurry to avoid burying ourselves in hand-knits. There are only so many scarves one knitter can use. 🐑

the 38th thing

Hope springs eternal.

ONCE UPON A TIME, a very nice knitter with a fair bit of experience decided to knit a sweater. She'd knit sweaters before. Despite some rather significant setbacks that she'd chosen to overlook (like the cardigan that didn't button in the front due to a misunderstanding about the size and location of her breasts, or the sweater with the very long arms resulting from a significant misread regarding the rate of decreases), the knitter had no qualms about beginning. For reasons to do with human hope and happiness, her past failure meant nothing to her.

She found a pattern she liked, found yarn she thought was excellent, conveniently forgot all the other projects she had underway, and launched into the sweater. She looked at the pattern and circled the instructions for her size. She read all the instructions and she even knit a swatch and, after some trial and error, got accurate gauge, both row and stitch.

Following the pattern, she cast on for the back, and she knit as the pattern indicated. She practiced due diligence and was a good and careful knitter. Maybe that was why she ignored the sweater when it started to look a little short. After all, when you do everything right, you should be able to have faith. When she reached the armholes and found that the thing was definitely too short, she overlooked the fact again and placed the armholes anyway. She knit to the recommended length. Despite the fact that the sweater was screaming, "Too short, way too short!" she kept going.

When the time came to sew up the shoulders and start the sleeves, the knitter finally had to acknowledge the shortness. She took a minute and made sure the sweater was the length the pattern indicated. It was. That was enough acknowledgment. She pressed on. She knit the sleeves carefully (thinking it was sort of funny that they were that much longer than the sweater body), but the whole time, some part of her, the hopeful part, did not suggest that she try on the sweater. Instead, it allowed her to check the pattern and suggested she re-measure the sweater to see if it matched the instructions. This rosy, sunny place inside her knitter's heart did not want her to try it on. That would have shattered the illusion that everything was perfect. The sweater was beautiful — beyond beautiful — and the knitter did not allow her suspicion that the thing was too freaking small to bloom. No way.

She finished the sleeves; she sewed the beast up. Then, she tried it on, and inevitably, with a sinking and shattered heart, she discovered that it was too short. She was absolutely shocked.

This is a peculiar trait of knitters. Whether knitting attracts people who are unusually optimistic or whether knitters are just plain delusional I don't know, but every knitter has demonstrated a version of this behavior. You know a piece of knitting is wrong, but you don't stop knitting. You see that the sleeve is too long, that the stitch is blue instead of red, that the yarn-over is in the wrong spot in your lace. You make a hat that will cover head and shoulders when finished or a sweater that will be short enough to display a middle-aged belly button to the world. You knit on, even when you see that you're creating a sweater with a neckline that accidentally plunges so low that Cher would feel risqué.

There are so many pieces of knitting that a knitter knows are wrong, knows are plainly unacceptable, even knows deep in her heart, are entirely unwearable. Yet you keep right on knitting. I don't know if it's denial, I don't know if it's optimism, and I certainly don't know if it's fantasy, but it proves that with knitters, hope always springs eternal.

the 39th thing

Goodness is its own reward.

SOMETIMES, IF I AM having a very, very bad day and much of humanity vexes me entirely, one of the only things that keeps me on the straight and narrow in this life is the knowledge that not all prisons have a knitting program. 🐑

the 40th thing

A friend in need is a friend indeed.

THE CULTURE OF KNIT IS RIFE with the stories of knitters helping one another. In fact, knitterly kindness is almost endemic.

It is not at all uncommon for a knitter (say, in Connecticut) who has run out of a discontinued yarn close to the end of a sweater to post a desperate request on an Internet mailing list asking if anyone can help her find a little bit more so she can finish. Once they read her plea, knitters worldwide will immediately implement an international stash search for the stuff in question, combing shops and closets far and wide. When the needed yarn is found in a stash in Germany, the knitter who locates it may happily mail the skein to the desperate knitter in Connecticut, often with absolutely no mention of compensation for the wool, time, or even postage.

I've known knitters to spend hours rescuing a knitter in technical trouble and to take the time to mail a book or a lost pattern. I can't tell you how often I've seen bilingual knitters translate patterns into other languages, almost always asking nothing for their time but the satisfaction of another good work knit. It is remarkable, when you consider the "you can't get something for nothing" attitude prevalent in the world right now, to find an entire subculture of people who are so likely help each other this way. It's refreshing.

Probably, this generosity and kindness is driven by empathy and understanding. Who among us can't imagine the absolute horror of knitting a whole sweater only to fall 13 yards short of yarn at the end of a sleeve? Or the sinking feeling of being far from home, stash, and a local yarn shop with nothing but free time to knit when you realize you don't have the pattern with you? Who among us, knowing the pain that knit-trauma can cause, would not respond to their pleas and rescue who we can? Most of us feel that if the ability to save even one of our fellow knitters from her wooly pain exists within us, we'd be remiss in failing to make the attempt.

I have learned, from watching the thousands of kindnesses enacted by knitters around the world, that there is little a knitter will not do for her fellow human in wooly need. Knitters' hearts are huge, their stashes open, and their generosity unbridled. A knitter's love and compassion for her fellow knitter knows no bounds.

Except at a yarn sale, when the gracious and generous knitter who just went through her stash and volunteered the needed skein of purple merino to a desperate fellow knitter now body-checks you into the sock-yarn display because that hand-painted laceweight she likes is 50 percent off and it looked you might get there before her.

Knitting is still trying to teach me . . .

THAT NO MATTER HOW WELL
YOU KNIT, LOOKING AT YOUR WORK
TOO CLOSELY ISN'T HELPFUL.
IT'S LIKE KISSING WITH YOUR
EYES OPEN: NOBODY LOOKS GOOD
THAT CLOSE UP.

the 41ˢᵗ thing

Birds of a feather flock together.

ALL MY KNITTING FRIENDS are just like me.
Every time I go to knit night at my local yarn
shop, I get to enjoy the wonderful feeling of
being one in a group of people with whom I have
a great deal in common.

There's Denny, a fiber artist and a mother
who makes her own bread, today knitting an
orange fascinator that will be trimmed with hundreds of itty-bitty pom-poms. Next to her is Dr.
Steph. Steph's an academic, a PhD mother of
young children, a professional who wears grown-
up clothes to work, and she's knitting a wire and
bead bracelet. Tonight, Jen is here. Jen's an
ex-stand-up comic expecting her first baby very
soon. She's knitting a bright baby sweater as she
sits on the steps in her Indian print sarong and
tank top. She has more time for knitting now that
she's too pregnant for long-distance canoe trips.

Jenna is a lawyer in a suit. Rachel is a business analyst. Alice is retired and cruising toward her eightieth birthday. Maria is a young professional from Mexico who always has a great dating story. Drea is on a budget so tight it squeaks, but Vanita can buy cashmere without blinking. Charlotte campaigned for the Conservative party, and Mina belongs to the Marijuana Party of Canada. Aven is a university professor. Sue is a university student. Aleta teaches high school English. Laura just graduated from college with a degree in linguistics. Ken does something with computers that I don't understand. Sarah is a stay-at-home mother who teaches Sunday school and is active in her church, and she's sitting next to Danny, who knits Fair Isle on the subway. Megan owns the shop, and our hearts, for giving us somewhere to hang out and do this. Me? I'm a fortyish writer with out-of-control hair and a personal loathing of housework that approaches spiritual levels. I'm the mother of three teen daughters.

I know that as I list the people around me at knit night, these individuals with whom I feel a tremendous sense of community, we don't sound much like birds of a feather. In fact, we sound like a zoo.

If you describe these knitters in conventional terms, using their politics, socioeconomic status, jobs, genders, or ages, it becomes obvious really quickly that we have almost nothing in common. It is not at all common to achieve this kind of wild diversity in a bunch of humans and still have them get along swimmingly. But with knitting groups it happens all the time.

I know, when I see groups of knitters like this, that some of us are people who wouldn't ordinarily be caught dead with each other (although we try not to talk about that, in case it breaks the spell we've cast). The only thing all of these knitters have in common is that we knit. That's it. Despite our diversity — diversity that causes wars (political and armed) in other places — at our knit night, nobody seems to notice. It's like the minute we take out our knitting, we identify first and foremost as knitters, and because of this, somehow even though we are an unlikely crew, all my knitting friends are just like me. We are birds of a feather. We flock together.

the 42nd thing

All's well that ends well.

THERE ARE A VERY GREAT MANY parallels between parenting and knitting. As I have journeyed on my own rather ragged path through both of them, I've learned that practicing one can help you be good at, or at least accepting of, the other.

In both knitting and parenting, the very hardest thing is that you have to do a lot of work for a long time before you have any idea at all if the project you are working on is going to be any good. With both parenting and knitting, you have to hang in there while you do the same things, over and over and over, always hoping for the best. (With knitting, it is stitches; with parenting, I believe it is either making lunches or saying No.)

With both things you have to have some faith that what you are working on will become beautiful and good, no matter what it looks like right now. With knitting, you try to up the odds that it's going to work: You choose good raw materials and knit gauge swatches. You watch other knitters and look at other sweaters. With parenting, it's exactly the same: You feed your kids (mostly) good food and put them to bed (mostly) on time. You read them stories and invest your time and energy in them, and you watch other people parent, learning from the things they do. You read knitting books and read parenting books, hoping the whole time that with enough work and effort, at the end of both processes, you'll get something good. The trouble is though, that with both knitting and parenting, there are no guarantees. Very good parents occasionally have kids that don't work out, and even the best knitters have turned out sweaters that were monstrosities. It is this uncertainty that has most of us a little nervous.

In these two stouthearted endeavors, it is, as it should be, parenting which is the really scary one. A badly knit sweater has never gotten hooked on meth and knocked over a liquor store, but all parents have had moments when they're terrified of what might happen next, or wonder if anything is going to work out in the end. This is where the similarities between knitting and parenting are like a reassuring friend. Knitting does work out most of the time. While you don't always get exactly what you were expecting, you almost always get something good. Knitting, like parenting, does seem sort of scary when your project is unfinished. It's hard to believe that the teenager slamming her door and the sweater with too-short sleeves are both going to end up being good things. Seeing that knitting works out if you can just stick with it can be balm to a frightened parent's heart. While you knit you can remember, things do get finished. They look bad because they are not finished, and all it takes is hope, time and work to finish them.

Knitting and parenting both start with pretty interesting raw materials, both take a long time to see if you're doing a good job, both have no performance appraisals and are done differently by everyone, and both, if you keep trying, end up with a finished something that will be a beautiful handmade surprise. 🐑

the 43rd *thing*

He who hesitates is lost.

OBVIOUSLY, THIS ONE IS ABOUT what we've all learned about managing our behavior at a yarn sale.

The yarn store is a very tempting place. Actually, the truth is that the yarn aisle at a regular store is a tempting place, and they don't even specialize. A yarn shop has no other product to distract you from the yarn or dilute your attention. To make matters worse, because a yarn shop sells only yarn, it is unlikely that you will even have brought a non-knitter or two with you, which is a shame, because nothing limits yarn-procurement behavior like a witness or someone who doesn't want to be there.

Since most of us have some trouble resisting temptation in a yarn shop on a good day, the mere idea of putting it on sale can make a normally sturdy knitter become a little crazed and slightly weak in the knees. It's an unfair set-up. Although we are comfortable and happy in a yarn shop, it is important to remember that the shop has one goal and one goal only: to sell you yarn. Luckily, most of us only have one goal in a yarn shop: to buy their yarn. A sale just ups the ante for both parties, because it introduces a dangerous element into yarn shopping: competition.

Almost all knitters recognize that buying yarn, especially yarn on sale, has competitive elements. First, there's the fact that there's a finite amount of yarn to be had; if there was an unlimited supply we wouldn't get so weird. Second, there's a limited amount of time in which to buy it. Third, there are going to be other knitters at the sale who know these first two things and are going to act on them the same way you are. If you're going to get what you want, you are going to need determination, and a plan.

Step 1: As soon as you know that the yarn store will be having a sale, arrange a trip to scout the location. Walk the store. Make notes about the position of yarn and the amount of yarn you'll purchase. If you feel it will help, make a map identifying the locale of your goal yarn. Leave your wallet at home so that the wool fumes can't get to you and weaken you so much that you purchase everything now that you're planning to buy at the sale later.

Step 2: The night before the sale, make a final list of what you want. Prioritize the list. It could be that another knitter will make it to the sock yarn you had in mind before you get there. If this happens, you don't want to waste time figuring out what your next move is. Make sure you note the amounts that you intend to purchase. You don't want to lose time to that super-quick Marie while you do math. Make plans to shop alone; your friends are only going to slow you down. Remember to get a good night's sleep.

Step 3: Show up at the shop on time. Be polite to the other knitters, but do not allow yourself to be distracted from your mission. John may seem like he is just being friendly, but more likely he's trying to keep you engaged in conversation while Rick empties out the worsted weight you had your eye on. Be suspicious. Some of these people are very experienced yarn shoppers competing at the Olympic level. Keep your head down, use your list and map and move quickly. Don't hesitate. Remember, you can always remove items from your basket later, but if you stand there thinking about whether or not you really want the 50-percent-off alpaca, then Alison is going to swoop in and scoop it up with all the precision of a strike missile.

Step 4: Don't underestimate the necessity of a good exit strategy. Many a fine knitter has gotten into a thing like this with no idea of how to get back out. Strike hard, strike fast, and make your getaway before things get complicated and you deviate from your plan and end up with sixteen skeins of a weird yellow wool that you have no idea what to do with.

Godspeed, and good luck. 🐑

Knitting is still trying to teach me . . .

THAT JUST BECAUSE IT'S DEEPLY

DISCOUNTED OR ON SALE,

IT ISN'T AUTOMATICALLY GOOD YARN.

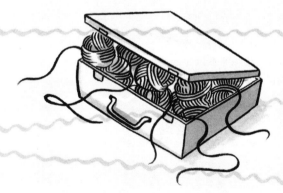

the 44th thing

My accomplishments are worth something.

I THINK THAT WE, AS KNITTERS, often diminish our skills. You make something beautiful, you sweat, you curse, you use a calculator and maim reams of graph paper, you rip back, you redo, you cultivate a skill . . . you hang tough and churn out something remarkable, something that's the result of hours and hours of your life and effort, and you feel pretty darned proud of yourself. Then someone walks up and says, "Wow! Did you make that? That's fantastic" or maybe "You're very talented," and then something comes over us and many of us knitters will turn, look the person dead in the eye and say, "No, no. It was easy."

Knitters so often complain that we aren't taken seriously as artisans and that knitting remains undervalued. This desire to make everything we do seem easy, our discomfort with the recognition of our talents, is not the way other people behave about their skills. Do lawyers say, "It was nothing"? Nope. They say, "That's $250 per hour. It took me a long time to learn how to do this." Artists don't say, "It was easy." They tell you how they learned to do what they do, or that this painting or sculpture is the result of a lifetime of experience and knowledge, and then because they have demonstrated respect for their efforts, so do we.

Knitting is a skill. The stuff we make is a fine reflection of the time we put into developing our skills. From now on, I am going to try to hold myself to a higher standard. I'm going to acknowledge that knitting is hard when it is. I'm not going to pretend a fancy lace shawl of my own fashioning just fell off my needles the way sweat falls off wrestlers and then go blushing myself off demurely into a corner.

The next time someone comes up to me and tells me my knitting is awesome, I'm going to look them in the eye and tell them the truth. When they say, "That's really beautiful" I'm going to take a deep breath, and I'm going to say, "Thank you. It was a challenge, but I did it."

the 45th thing

I am very lucky.

RECENTLY, I BOUGHT YARN. I preceded this rather unremarkable event by checking my bank account, thinking over what I could afford to spend. I then forked over the cash. Then I read something from the World Bank that shook me up pretty badly. The population of the world at the time of this writing is apparently about 6.7 billion. According to the World Bank, 3 billion of those people are living on less than $2 a day. Of these, 1.3 billion are making a go of it on less than $1 per day. These facts stayed with me as I squirreled my new yarn away among its compatriots in my stash.

I have a stash. It's a good one too, and I don't feel bad or guilty about it. In fact, to be entirely honest . . . I love it. There's yarn in there that I would totally take with me in a house fire. Knitting has taught me that there is a deep and grand satisfaction in having the means around me to occupy myself and to make things for the people I love that keep them warm, both literally and spiritually. I think that knitting is profoundly satisfying and worthy and it's enriched my life tremendously. I wouldn't want to be without it even as it takes up most of my extra cash and closet space.

I admit that my love for yarn means that I'm occasionally frustrated when I run out of space for my yarn collection in my tiny house — and I'm way more than occasionally frustrated when I can't afford to buy something like the worsted-weight cashmere from my favorite hand-dyer. I have to be reasonable, though, because like just about every knitter, I have a yarn budget. I have to make choices about paying the rent, buying food. I must remember that when the bills for my daughters' educations start rolling in, the fact that I have a well-appointed yarn closet and they have very beautiful mittens won't mean a thing if Mamma blew the whole household savings on stash enhancement.

The World Bank indicates that most North Americans fall into the 1 percent of the world's population that has about 80 percent of the world's money. Even though that gives me a pang of guilt, I don't think the World Bank is out to make me feel horrible about how much I have. In fact, I don't think they were considering knitters at all when they came up with that statistic. The goal is simply to point out inequity, and I'm sure they hope that reading their statistics results in at least a small shift in the way people like us think sometimes.

It turns out that knitting is a luxury, and buying yarn (even cheap yarn) or having time to knit (even five minutes) or simply sitting in my house (even my very small house) with that warm, soft yarn in my hands is a sign that I am extraordinarily rich and fortunate. Knowing this means that I'm going to try to remember the very best things knitting has taught me so far. Sitting here screwing up this sweater means something. It means I lead a very good life. I am lucky. I am fortunate.

I am a knitter. 🐑

With thanks to:

My husband, Joe, who tries so hard to stay out of my office.

My daughters, Amanda, Megan, and Samantha, who don't try to stay out of my office, but I love anyway.

My mum, Bonnie, who loaned me the use of her kitchen floor during the last phase of this book when I used up all the space in my office.

My brother, Ian, who helped me build my office.

My sister, Erin, my nephew, Hank, and my sister-in-law, Ali, for having nothing to do with my office.

My agent, Linda Roghaar, for having (thank goodness) an office that runs more efficiently than mine.

My dear friends Lene, Rachel, Denny, Tina, Cassandra, and Ken . . . who all somehow know when it's time I should leave my office, and how to encourage me to stay in there until my work is done.

Molly Wolf, for perspective on the work that came out of the office.

Pam Art, Deborah Balmuth, Jayme Hummer, and everyone else at Storey Publishing who gave me a reason to have an office at all . . .

and finally, many, many heartfelt thanks to all the knitters I meet, both "live" and "virtual." You make the time that I sit in my office totally worth it, and not many people can say that.